Church Hymnal

Tennessee Music and Printing Company
A Division of Pathway Press
P. O. Box 2250
Cleveland, Tennessee 37320-2250

© Copyright 1951 (Renewal, 1979) by Tennessee Music and Printing Company.
All Rights Reserved.

It's Just Like Heaven

I'm Free Again

I Want to Know More About My Lord

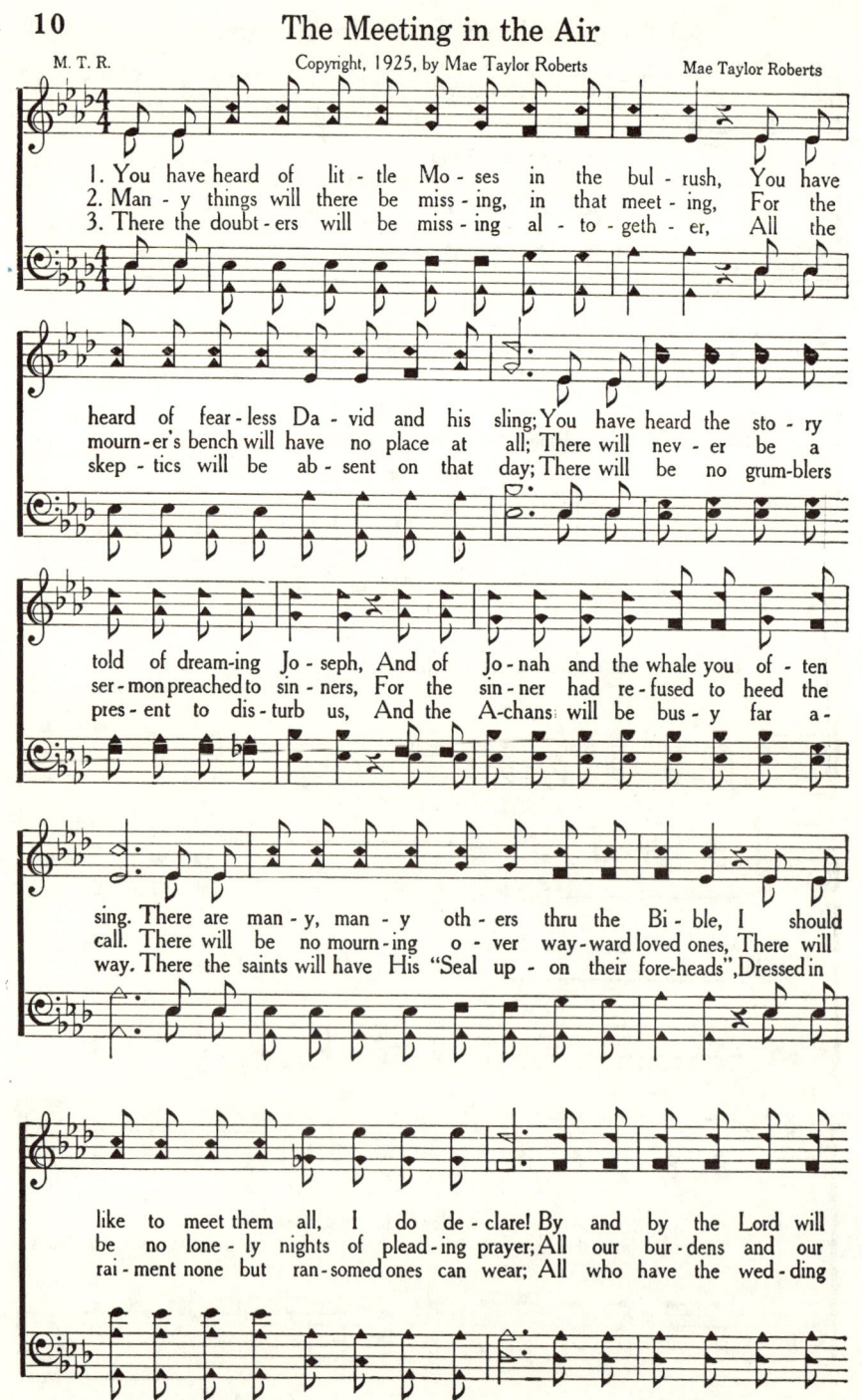

When He Calls I'll Fly Away

When He Calls I'll Fly Away

13

I'll Meet You In Morning

Sit down by the riv-er sit down by the riv-er
sit down by the riv-er and with
rap-ture our "auld" ac-quaintance re-new, Know me in the morn-
rap-ture "auld" acquaintance re - new, You'll know
ing, know me in the morn-ing, smiles that I wear
me in the morn-ing by the smiles that I
smiles that I wear, Meet you in the morn-ing, meet you in the morn-ing,
wear, When I meet you in the morn-ing,
Cit-y cit-y built, that cit-y built four square.
In the cit-y that is built four square.

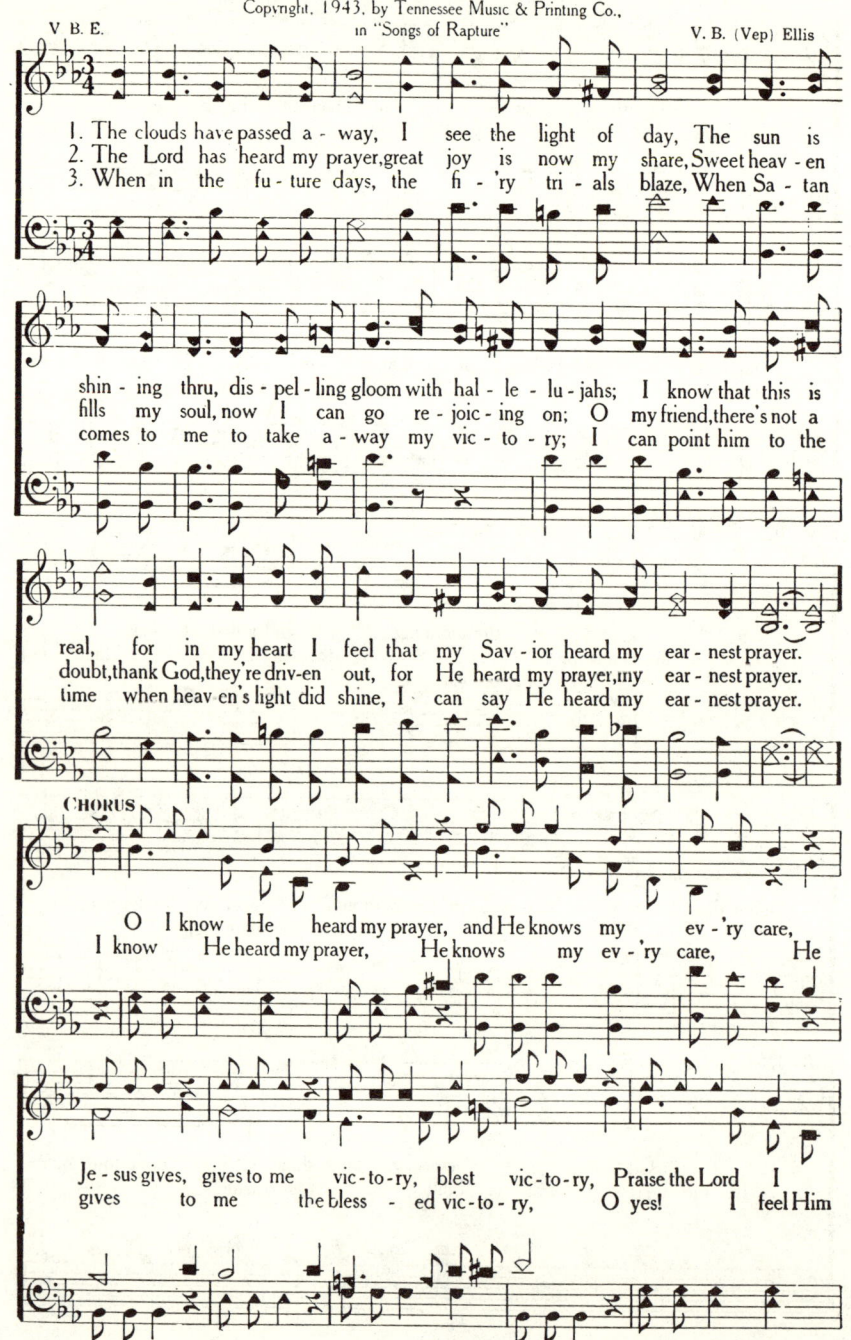

I Know He Heard My Prayer

Looking For a City

19

He's My King

A. M. P.
Copyright, 1936, Adger M. Pace, owner
Adger M. Pace

1. I have a Friend Divine, walking with me, Making my pathway shine, Mighty is He; Jesus, the One I love, gladly I sing Praises to Him above, He is my King.
2. I have a Saviour dear, talking with me, He is so very near, seems I can see; Over life's rugged way to Him I cling, He is my guide and stay, Jesus my King.
3. I have the Holy Ghost living in me, He is my Royal Host, faithful is He; Filling me with His love, so I may sing Praises to Christ above, He is my King.

CHORUS

He's my King, and reigns forevermore,
He's my blessed King,
He's my King, forevermore, I love Him,
He's my King to worship and adore, Oh, I dearly
He's my heav'nly King
He's my King whom I adore,

He's My King

love Him, There is none a - bove Him, Won - der - ful is
Won - der - ful is
He; He's my King, let
He; this might - y King of glo - ry, He's my bless - ed King,
He's my King, let
all the world pro - claim, He's my King of
He's my heav'n - ly King
all pro - claim it loud - ly, He's my King of
roy - al, Ho - ly fame, When I get to glo - ry, I will sing the
Ho - - ly fame,
sto - ry, Of His love for me.
Of His love for me, His love for me.

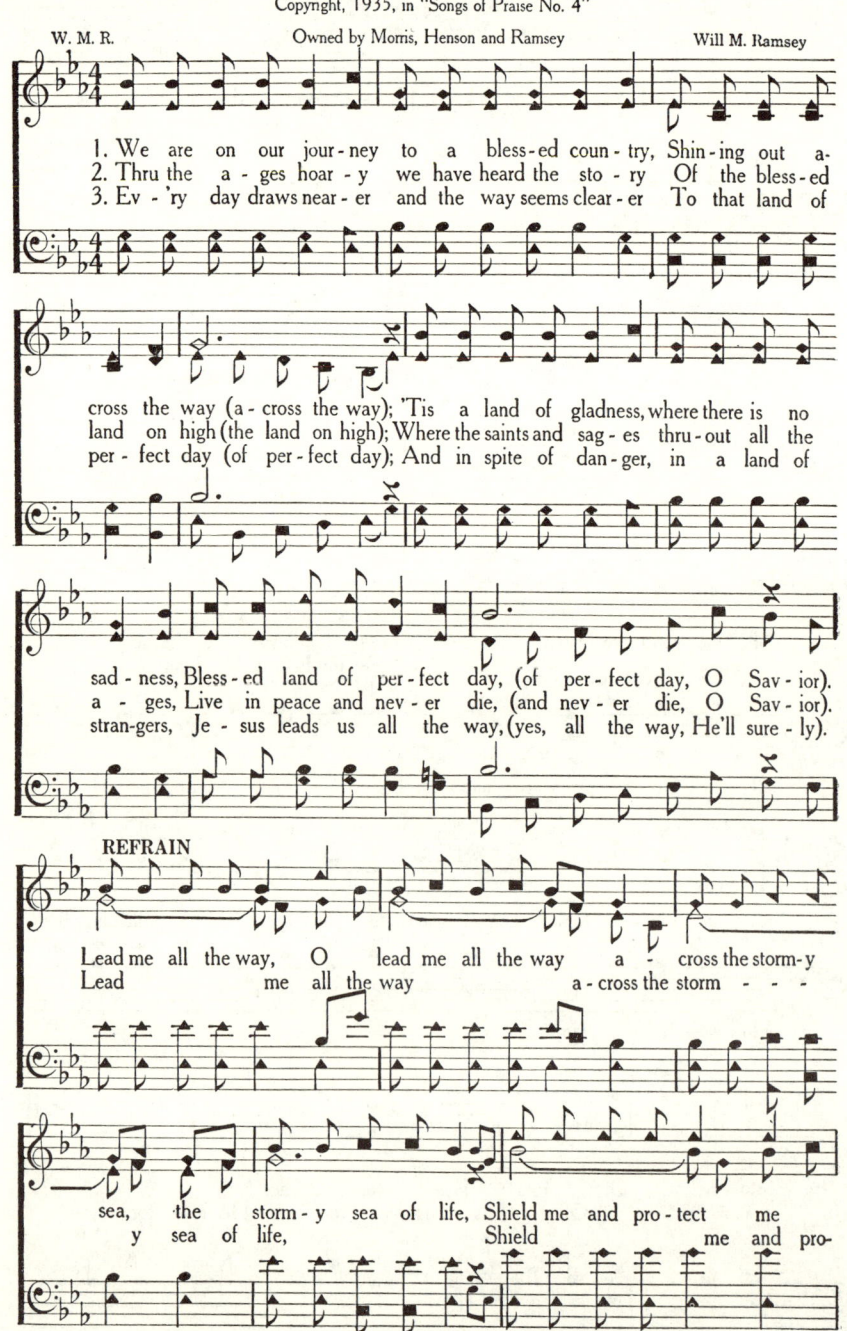

The Land of Perfect Day

Be Ready To Go

25

Take a Moment and Live

It's a Grand And a Glorious Feeling

30 We'll Soon Be Done With Troubles and Trials

(Dedicated to my father and mother, Mr. and Mrs. J. T. Derricks.—C. D.)

C. D.   Copyright, 1934, by The Stamps-Baxter Music Co., in "Pearls of Paradise"   Cleavant Derricks

1. Some of these days I'm go - ing home where no sor - rows ev - er come,
2. Kin - dred and friends now wait for me, soon their fac - es I shall see,
3. I shall be - hold His bless - ed face, I shall feel His match - less grace,

We'll soon be done with trou-bles and tri - als;
We'll soon be done,   trou-bles and tri - als;

Safe from heart-ache, pain and care, we shall all that glo - ry share,
'Tis a home of life so fair and we'll all be gath - ered there,
O what peace and joy sub - lime in that home of love di - vine,

Sit down be - side my Je - sus,   sit down and
And I'm gon - na   Lord, I'm gon - na

CHORUS

rest a lit - tle while.   We'll soon be done with trou-bles and
We'll soon be done,

We'll Soon Be Done With Troubles and Trials

★ After last only.

I Will Slip Away Home

If We Never Meet Again   37

There's a Guiding Hand

way, By this hand I'm safe-ly hid-ing
rough and wea-ry way, By this faithful hand I am safe-ly hid-ing
from the temp - - - - - ter day by day; When the
from the temp-ter hide ev-'ry pass-ing day;
storms a-round are beat-ing, It will make
When the howling storms are a-round me beat-ing, It will make the
the sun to shine, O what joy it is in
sun O so bright to shine, What a wondrous joy
meet-ing, With the hand of love di-vine.
joy it is in meet-ing, With the guiding hand of love di-vine, of love di-vine.

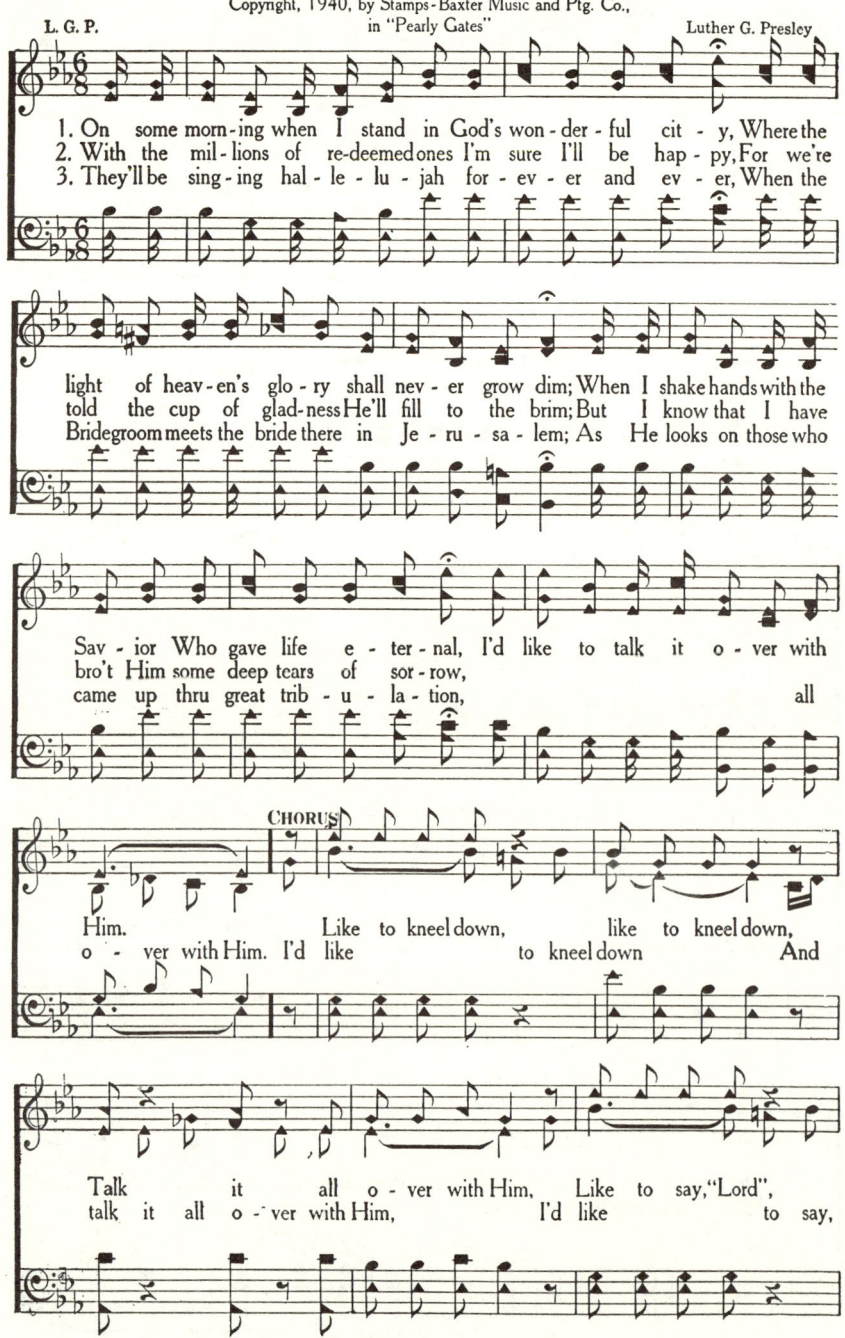

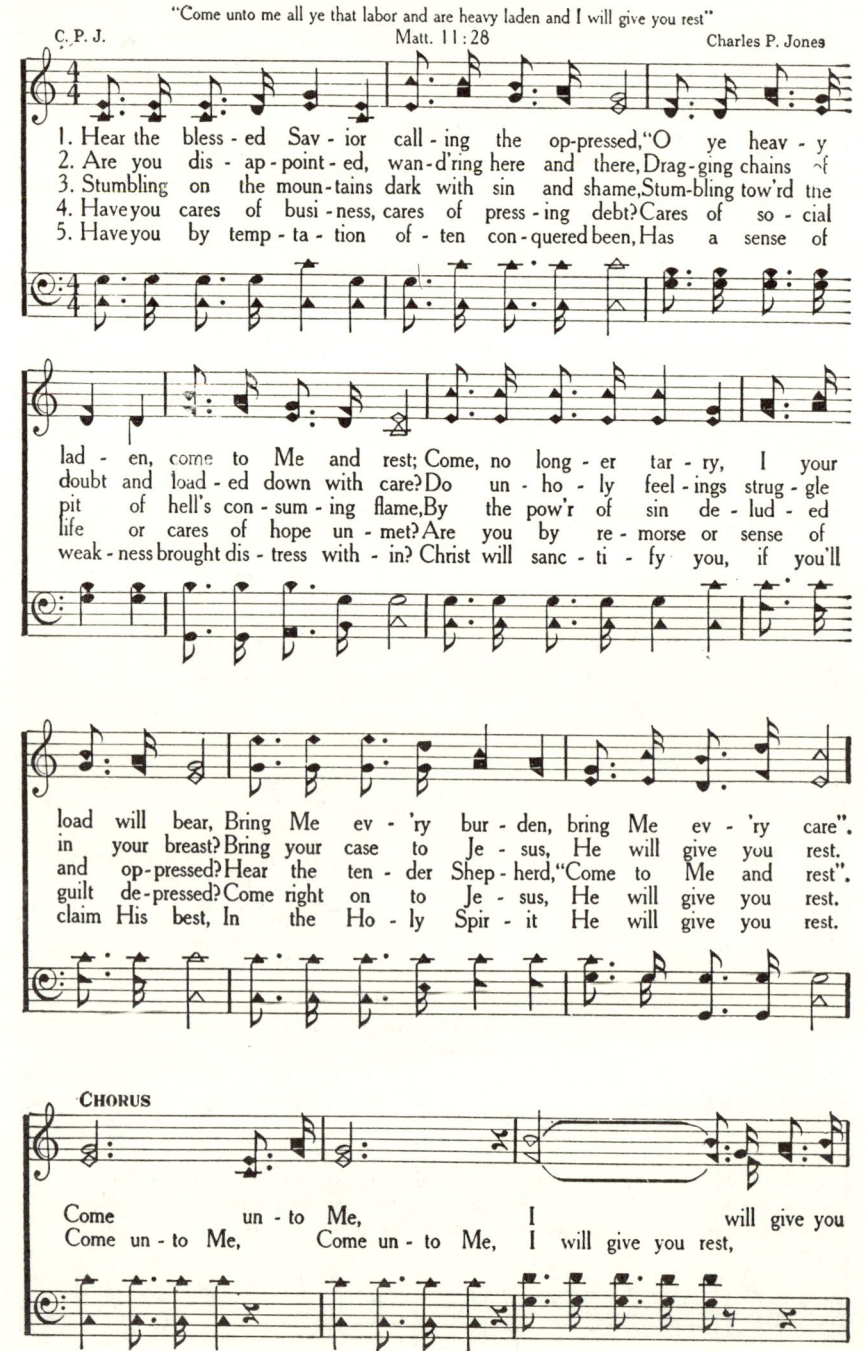

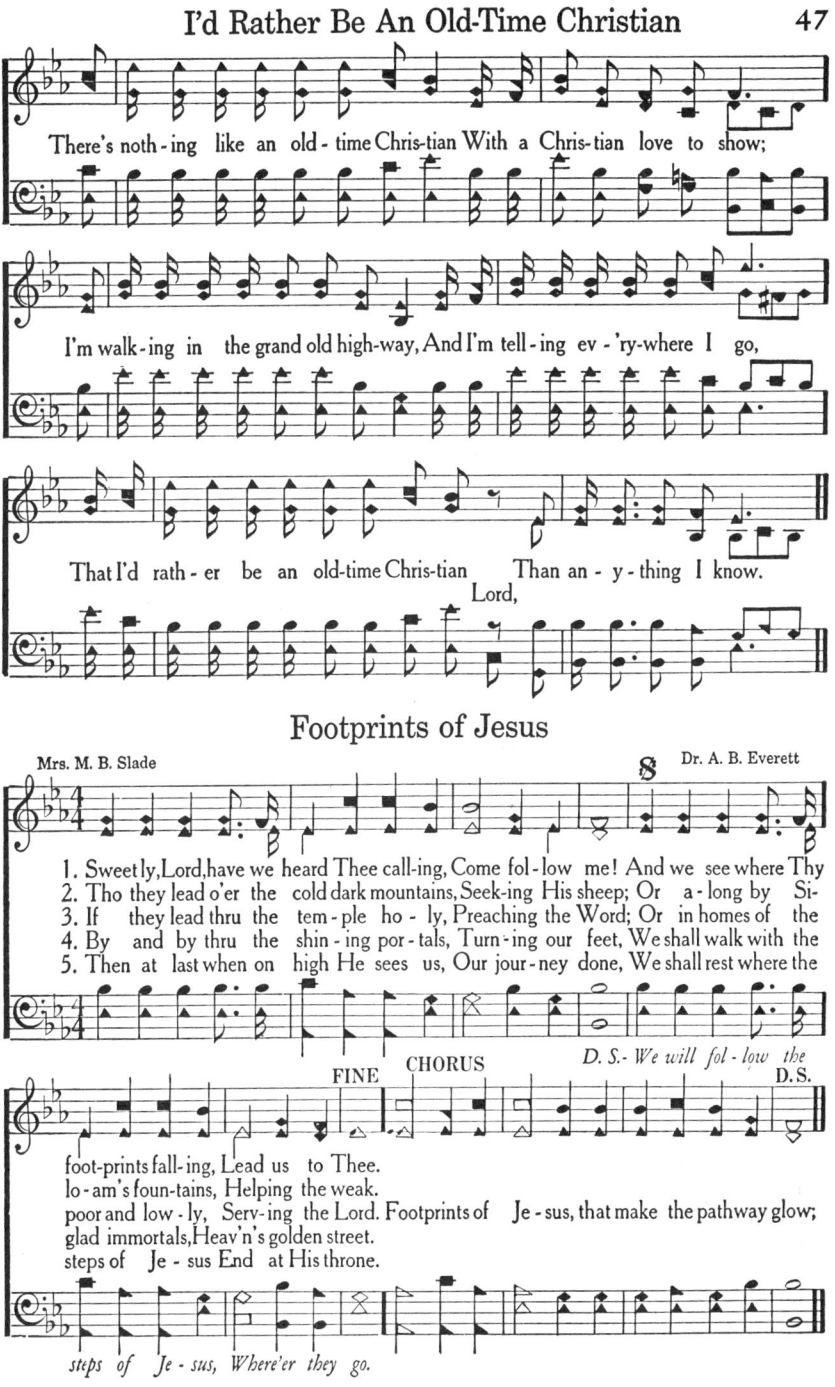

Jesus, Hold My Hand

A. E. B.  Albert E. Brumley

1. As I trav-el thru this pil-grim land There is a Friend who walks with me,
2. Let me trav-el in the light di-vine That I may see the bless-ed way;
3. When I wan-der thru the val-ley dim To-ward the set-ting of the sun,

Leads me safe-ly thro' the sink-ing sand, It is the Christ of Cal-va-ry;
Keep me that I may be whol-ly Thine And sing redemption's song some day;
Lead me safe-ly to a land of rest If I a crown of life have won;

This would be my pray'r, dear Lord, each day To help me do the best I can, For I
I will be a sol-dier brave and true And ev-er firm-ly take a stand, As I
I have put my faith in Thee, dear Lord, That I may reach the gold-en strand, There's no

need Thy light to guide me day and night Bless-ed Je-sus, hold my hand.
on-ward go and dai-ly meet the foe, Bless-ed Je-sus, hold my hand.
oth-er friend on whom I can de-pend, Bless-ed Je-sus, hold my hand.

CHORUS

Bless-ed Je-sus, hold my hand, Yes, I need Thee ev-'ry hour,
Je-sus, hold my hand, I need Thee ev-'ry hour,

He Will Be With Me

O He will keep, keep me His own each step of the way, each step of the way;
He will keep me His own ev-'ry step of the way;

Till at the gate, heaven's bright gate, the face of my Lord and King I shall see,
Till at heav-en's bright gate His dear face I shall see,

Sure-ly I know Je-sus, my Friend, will be with me.
I know my Re-deem-er will ev-er be walk-ing with me.

Jesus Loves Even Me

P. P. B. "God is Love".-John, 4: 8 P. P. Bliss

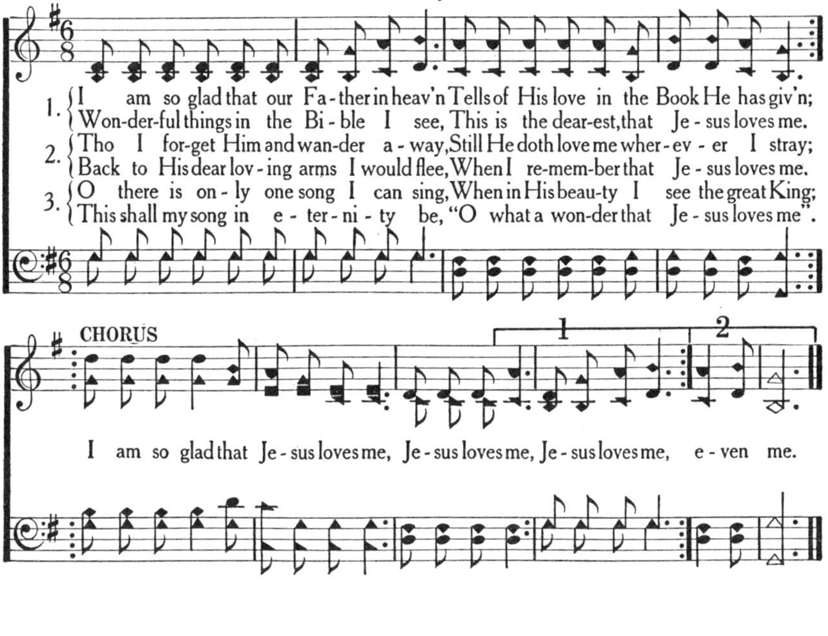

1. { I am so glad that our Fa-ther in heav'n Tells of His love in the Book He has giv'n;
    Won-der-ful things in the Bi-ble I see, This is the dear-est, that Je-sus loves me.
2. { Tho I for-get Him and wan-der a-way, Still He doth love me wher-ev-er I stray;
    Back to His dear lov-ing arms I would flee, When I re-mem-ber that Je-sus loves me.
3. { O there is on-ly one song I can sing, When in His beau-ty I see the great King;
    This shall my song in e-ter-ni-ty be, "O what a won-der that Je-sus loves me".

CHORUS

I am so glad that Je-sus loves me, Je-sus loves me, Je-sus loves me, e-ven me.

60. His Love And Glory Are Mine

James Rowe — Copyright, 1926, in "Special Songs" No. 5 H. F. Morris, owner — Homer F. Morris

1. The Sav-ior now walks with me and sweet-ly He talks with me, As up-ward to glo-ry I go; And dai-ly I sing to Him and fond-ly I cling to Him, Be-cause I am lov-ing Him so. With mer-cy in-fold-ing me and pow-er up-hold-ing me, I nev-er com-plain or re-pine; No mat-ter what may be-tide, as-sur-ance will still a-bide,

2. He's ev-er de-fend-ing me, rich bless-ings is send-ing me, While walk-ing the heav-en-ly way; And noth-ing ap-pall-eth me, no e-vil be-fall-eth me, In safe-ty I'm walk-ing each day. For nev-er re-prov-ing me, but lead-ing and lov-ing me, He caus-eth the home-path to shine; And sweet-ly I'm prais-ing Him, to sin-ners up-rais-ing Him, His love and His glo-ry are mine,

3. Where endeth the sto-ry land be-gin-eth the glo-ry land, Where ev-er with Him I shall be; Thru Je-sus all-glo-ri-ous, for-ev-er vic-to-ri-ous, The life-crown is com-ing to me. So dai-ly I walk with Him and sweet-ly I talk with Him, My bless-ed Re-deem-er di-vine; And ev-er my song shall be His won-der-ful love for me,

His Love And Glory Are Mine

61

REFRAIN

Ev - er is mine, glo - ry I shine,
His love for - ev - er is mine and with His glo - ry I shine, And so His

Good-ness I tell, prais-es I swell; Home-ward I go,
good-ness I tell and hap-py prais-es I swell; As on to heav - en I go,

hap-py to know, Glo - ry for - ev - er is mine.
re - joic - ing ev - er to know, His love and glo - ry for - ev - er are mine.(ev - er mine).

Abide With Me

H. F. Lyte   Wm. H. Monk

1. A - bide with me! Fast falls the e - ven-tide, The dark-ness deepens, Lord, with me a - bide!
2. Swift to its close ebbs out life's lit - tle day, Earth's joys grow dim, its glo-ries pass a - way;
3. I need Thy presence ev'ry passing hour, What but Thy grace can foil the tempter's pow'r?
4. Hold Thou Thy cross before my closing eyes, Shine thro' the gloom, and point me to the skies;

When oth - er help-ers fail, and comforts flee, Help of the helpless, oh, a - bide with me!
Change and de - cay in all a - round I see; O Thou who changest not, a - bide with me!
Who, like Thyself, my guide and stay can be? Thru cloud and sunshine, O a - bide with me!
Heav'n's morning breaks and earth's vain shadows flee! In life, in death, O Lord, a - bide with me!

It Won't Be Long

Till I shall join the ransomed throng;
Till I shall join the throng, hap-py ransomed throng;
In heav'n a-bove, (in heav'n a-bove), with the ones I love, (with those I love),
Oh, praise the Lord, it won't be long. (it won't be long).

Jesus, Lover of My Soul

Charles Wesley
S. B. Marsh

1. {Je-sus, lov-er of my soul, Let me to Thy bos-om fly;
   {While the near-er wa-ters roll, While the tem-pest still is high.}
2. {Oth-er ref-uge have I none, Hangs my help-less soul on Thee;
   {Leave, ah, leave me not a-lone, Still sup-port and com-fort me.}
3. {Plen-t'ous grace with Thee is found, Grace to cov-er all my sin;
   {Let the heal-ing streams a-bound, Make and keep me pure with-in.}

D. C.-Safe in-to the ha-ven guide, O re-ceive my soul at last.
D. C.-Cov-er my de-fense-less head, With the shad-ow of Thy wing.
D. C.-Spring Thou up with-in my heart, Rise to all e-ter-ni-ty.

Hide me, O my Sav-ior hide, Till the storm of life is past;
All my trust on Thee is stayed, All my help from Thee I bring;
Thou of life the foun-tain art, Free-ly let me take of Thee;

Wonderful Grace of Jesus

grace, all suf-fi- - - cient for me, for e-ven me;
sparkling like a foun-tain, All suf-fi-cient grace for e-ven me,

Broad-er than the scope of my trans-gres - sions, Great-er far than all my sin and
gres-sions, sing it!

shame, O mag-ni-fy the precious name of Je-sus, Praise His name!
my sin and shame,

Where He Leads Me

E. W. Blandly Copyright, 1890, by J. S. Norris. Used by permission. J. S. Norris

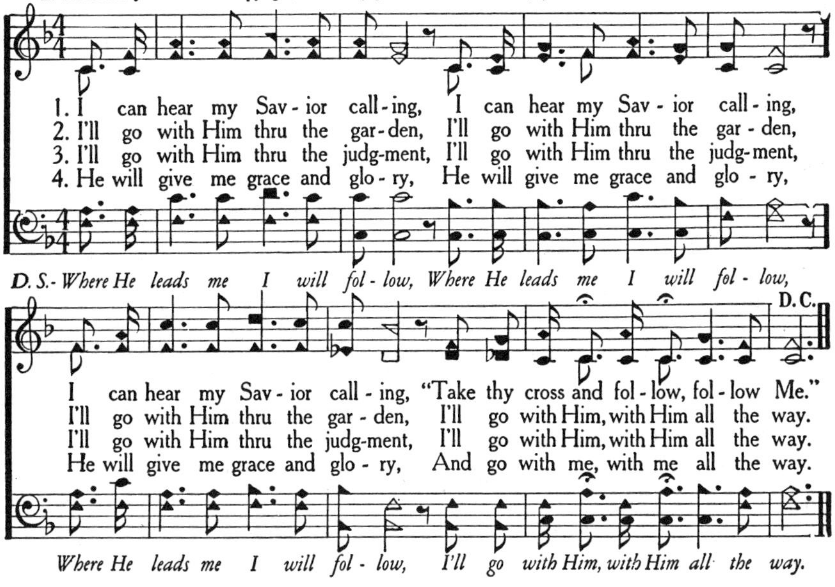

1. I can hear my Sav-ior call-ing, I can hear my Sav-ior call-ing,
2. I'll go with Him thru the gar-den, I'll go with Him thru the gar-den,
3. I'll go with Him thru the judg-ment, I'll go with Him thru the judg-ment,
4. He will give me grace and glo-ry, He will give me grace and glo-ry,

D. S.-Where He leads me I will fol-low, Where He leads me I will fol-low,

I can hear my Sav-ior call-ing, "Take thy cross and fol-low, fol-low Me."
I'll go with Him thru the gar-den, I'll go with Him, with Him all the way.
I'll go with Him thru the judg-ment, I'll go with Him, with Him all the way.
He will give me grace and glo-ry, And go with me, with me all the way.

Where He leads me I will fol-low, I'll go with Him, with Him all the way.

The Lord Is With Me

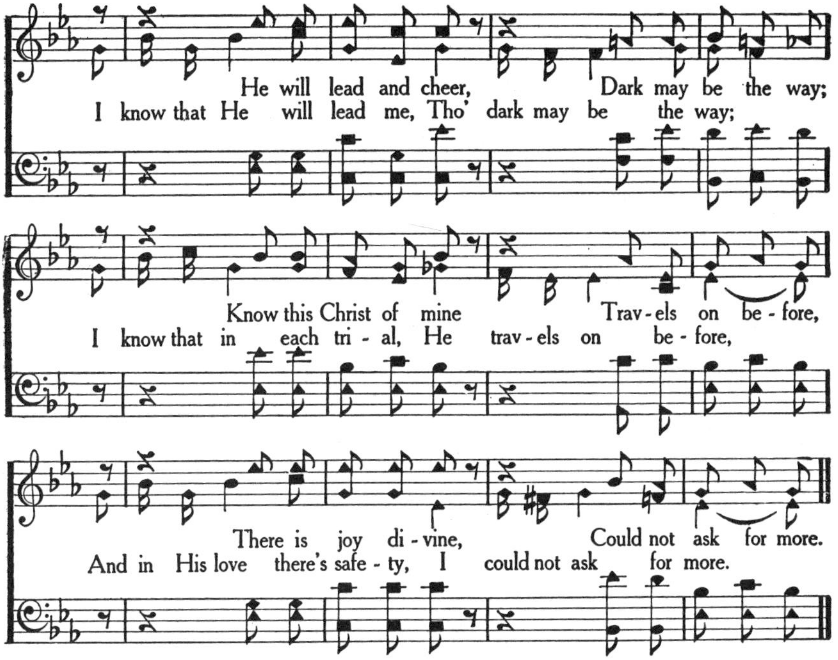

Take My Life, and Let It Be

F. R. Havergal

Wm. B. Bradbury

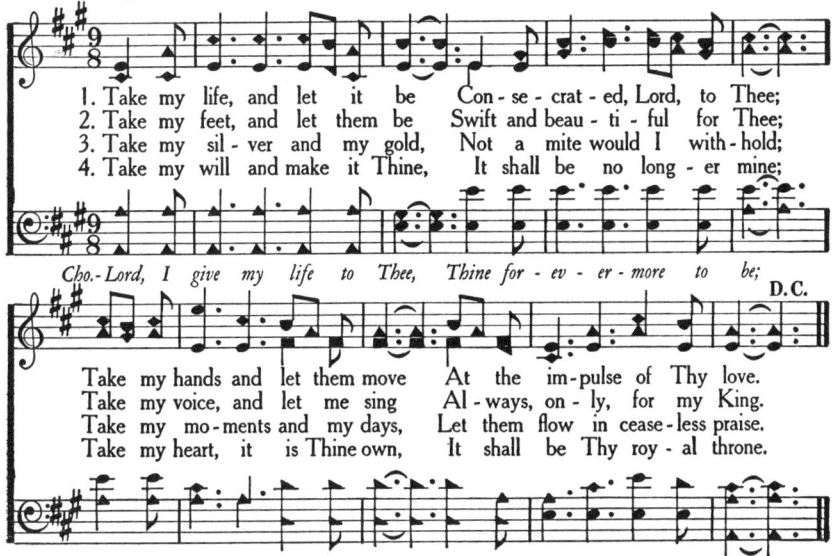

82 Singing of Love Divine

J. B. P.  J. B. Paris

1. Sing-ing of love di-vine from day to day, on-ward to glo-ry I go,
2. Sing-ing till He shall call me o-ver there then with my dear ones a-gain,
3. 'Twill not be ver-y long till I shall go, yon-der to be with my King,

Trav-'ling the glo-ry line, love lights the way, To that blest home-land I know.
Tear-drops will nev-er fall, nev-er a care, In heaven's love-ly do-main.
There with the happy throng, some day I know, Sweeter the songs I shall sing.

CHORUS

Prais - - - ing Je-sus my King,
Ev-er prais-ing, ev-er prais-ing, King of glo-ry
Ev - - - er prais - - ing

Sing-ing of love so di-vine; Tho' days be dark or drear
of love di-vine; He keeps me

His love will al-ways cheer and guide me safe-ly a-cross the line.
.the dan-ger line.

Singing of Love Divine

Soon I'll be with that throng
I'll be hap-py, O so hap-py o - ver yon - der
Soon I'll be with

sing-ing a won-der-ful song, a hap-py song in glo-ry; Sit-ting at Je-sus' feet

my joy will be com-plete, Some glad time.
Sweet-ly sing-ing, ev - er sing-ing some glad time.
Some glad hap - - py time.

Rock of Ages

A. M. Toplady (Toplady) Thos. Hastings
FINE

1. Rock of A - ges, cleft for me, Let me hide my - self in Thee;
2. Could my tears for - ev - er flow, Could my zeal no lan - guor know,
3. While I draw this fleet-ing breath, When mine eyes shall close in death,

D. C.- Be of sin the dou - ble cure, Save from wrath and make me pure.
In my hand no price I bring, Sim - ply to Thy cross I cling.
Rock of A - ges, cleft for me, Let me hide my - self in Thee.
D.C.

Let the wa - ter and the blood, From Thy wound-ed side which flowed,
These for sin could not a - tone; Thou must save, and Thou a - lone;
When I rise to worlds un-known, And be - hold Thee on Thy throne,

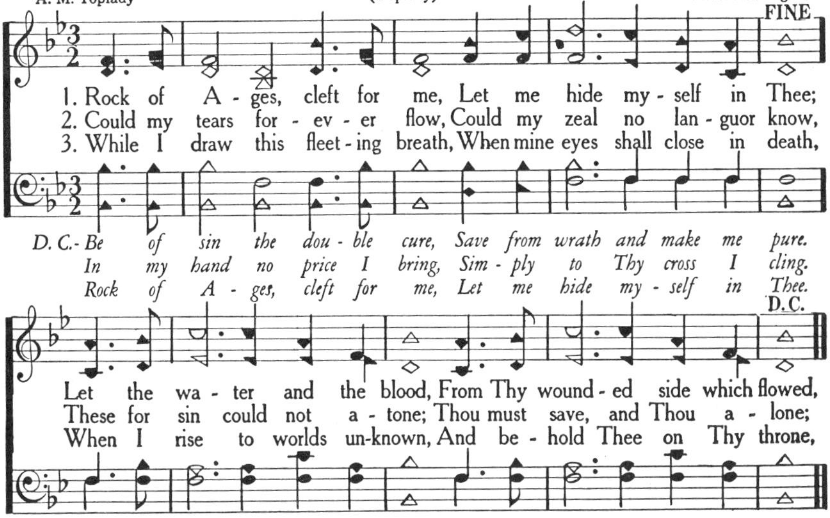

88. I'm Going That Way

James Rowe   L. B. Register, Greenville, Fla., owner. By per.   L. B. Register

1. I've heard of a land of joy and peace and won-der-ful light, (and won-der-ful light),
2. The glo-ri-ous news I tell and sing, as I on-ward go, (as on-ward I go);
3. I know I shall meet Him at the gate, when tri-als are past, (when tri-als are past),

A beau-ti-ful place of man-sions fair and skies ev-er bright, (and skies ev-er bright),
That those who are still a-stray in sin my Sav-ior may know, (my Sav-ior may know),
I know I shall meet Him face to face in glo-ry at last, (in glo-ry at last);

Where all who be-lieve the Sav-ior dear, for-ev-er shall stay, (for-ev-er shall stay),
I want them to sing His praise a-bove, some beau-ti-ful day, (some beau-ti-ful day),
And O I be-lieve that when we meet "well done" He will say, ("well done" He will say),

And hav-ing been saved by grace di-vine, I'm go-ing that way.
For glo-ry to Him who died for me, I'm go-ing that way.
For trust-ing His soul-re-deem-ing love, I'm go-ing that way.

CHORUS

I'm go-ing that way (I'm on that way); I'm go-ing that way, (I'm go-ing that way),
I'm cling-ing to Him, (I cling to Him), and nev-er to stray, (and nev-er to stray),

I'm Going That Way

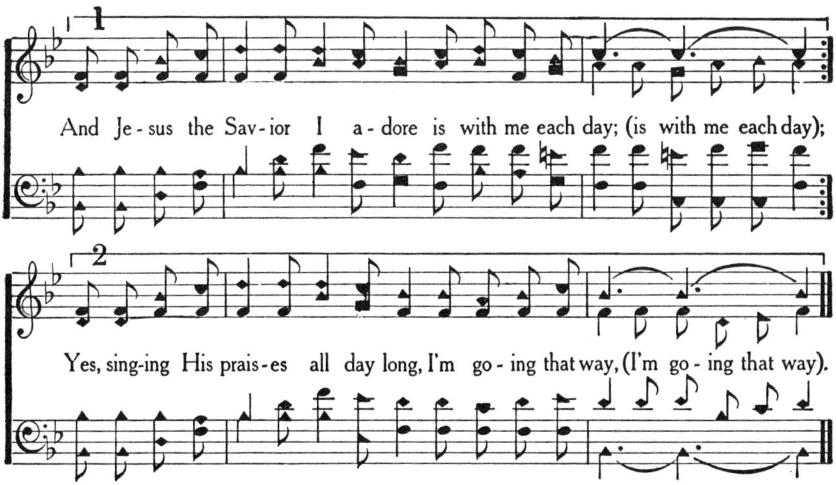

And Je-sus the Sav-ior I a-dore is with me each day; (is with me each day);

Yes, sing-ing His prais-es all day long, I'm go-ing that way, (I'm go-ing that way).

The Great Reaping Day

R. E. W.   Owned by R. E. Winsett, Dayton, Tenn.   R. E. Winsett

1. There is com-ing a day when to judgment we'll go There to reap as in life we've sown,
2. Ev-'ry day pass-ing by you are sow-ing the seed Fruits of life or of death will bear,
3. If you'd win life e-ter-nal there's no time to lose, Look a-round you, the fields are white,
4. Ev-'ry act you per-form is a seed to some one, For the in-flu-ence will ne'er die,

Death e-ter-nal we'll reap if we sow to the flesh, Heaven's joys then will nev-er be known.
When you reap what you sow to that land may you go, To that bright happy home o-ver there.
Go ye forth to the field, sow and reap golden grain, Soon will fall the dark shadows of night.
Then be care-ful each day what you do, what you say, For you'll meet it a-gain by and by.

D. S.- O the joy on that day when we hear Je-sus say, Come, ye bless-ed, a crown you have won.

CHORUS

May we sow right-eous seed for the reap-ing, Which is com-ing to ev-'ry one,

I'm In a New World

new, ev-er since that hap-py day, He o-pened up my blind-ed
things are new, glad day,

eyes and then I had a great sur-prise, I'm in a new
liv-ing in a

D.S.

I'm Glad I Counted the Cost

Words and air by W. J. Henry Harmony by A. L. B.

1. When first I start-ed to seek the Lord, I'm glad I count-ed the cost;
2. I laid my sor-rows at Je-sus' feet, I'm glad I count-ed the cost;
3. I've bid fare-well to this world of sin, I'm glad I count-ed the cost;
4. Al-though the tri-als seem hard to bear, I'm glad I count-ed the cost;
5. 'Twill not be long till the Lord shall come, I'm glad I count-ed the cost;

FINE.

I ful'-ly meas-ured to Je-sus' word,
And now I've pleas-ures so pure and sweet,
And now my Je-sus a-bides with-in, I'm glad I count-ed the cost.
I now my bur-dens with Je-sus share,
And bear my soul to that heav'n-ly home,

D. S.- *And now my treas-ures are in the skies,*

CHORUS D.S.

I've paid the price and ob-tained the prize, He saved my soul that was lost;

Lord Lead Me On

walk the ho-ly way; Tho' friends for-sake,
want to walk the ho-ly way; Tho' friends for-sake,

me all a-lone, I ask Thee Lord,
me all a-lone, I ask Thee Lord to lead me on.

Jesus Saves

Priscilla J. Owens Copyright, 1882, by John J. Hood Wm. J. Kirkpatrick

1. We have heard the joy-ful sound, Je-sus saves, Je-sus saves; Spread the glad-ness
2. Waft it on the roll-ing tide, Je-sus saves, Je-sus saves; Tell to sin-ners
3. Sing a-bove the bat-tle's strife, Je-sus saves, Je-sus saves; By His death and
4. Give the winds a might-y voice, Je-sus saves, Je-sus saves; Let the na-tions

all a-round, Je-sus saves, Je-sus saves, Bear the news to ev-'ry land, Climb the
far and wide, Je-sus saves, Je-sus saves; Sing, ye is-lands of the sea, Ech-o
end-less life, Je-sus saves, Je-sus saves; Sing it soft-ly thru the gloom, When the
now re-joice, Je-sus saves, Je-sus saves; Shout sal-va-tion full and free, High-est

steeps and cross the waves, Onward, 'tis our Lord's command, Je-sus saves, Je-sus saves.
back, ye o-cean caves, Earth shall sing her ju-bi-lee, Je-sus saves, Je-sus saves.
heart for mer-cy craves, Sing in tri-umph o'er the tomb, Je-sus saves, Je-sus saves.
hill and deep-est caves, This our song of vic-to-ry, Je-sus saves, Je-sus saves.

Lift Me Up Above the Shadows

101

let me stand on the moun - - - - tain tops of
lift me up and let me stand on the moun-tain tops of glo - ry, on the
glo - ry, Let me dwell in Beu-lah land.
moun-tain tops of glo - ry, Let me dwell in Beu-lah land, O let me dwell in Beulah land.

His Blood is on My Soul

R. E. W.   Owned by R. E. Winsett   R. E. Winsett

1. Dear Je - sus all my sins for - gave, And washed and made me whole,
2. The temp - ter can - not o - ver-come, Or gain the least con - trol,
3. I have His Spir - it now with - in, My life in His con - trol,
4. I am de - ter - mined by His grace To reach bright heav-en's goal,

I have sweet peace and joy with - in, His blood is on my soul.
I have God's ev - er - last - ing seal, Christ's blood is on my soul.
I'm read - y for the crown - ing day, His blood is on my soul.
And reign with Je - sus on His throne, His blood is on my soul.

D. S.—I rest se - cure - ly in His hand, His blood is on my soul.

CHORUS   D.S.

His blood is on my soul, (my soul), His blood is on my soul;

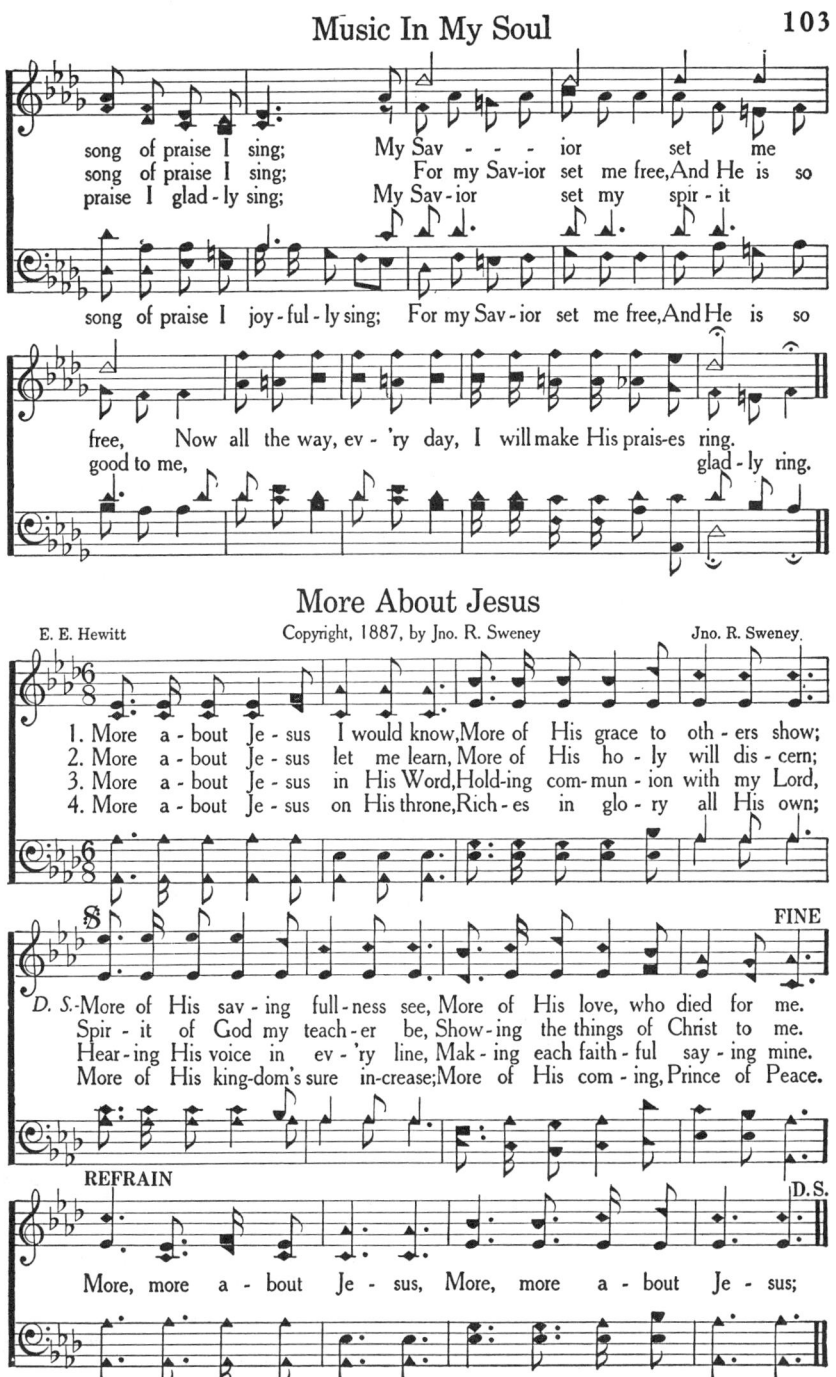

110 Heaven's Jubilee

Adger M. Pace
Copyright, 1939, G. T. Speer, owner
G. T. Speer

1. Some glad morn-ing we shall see Je-sus in the air, Com-ing aft-er you and me, joy is ours to share; What re-joic-ing there will be when the saints shall rise, Head-ed for that ju-bi-lee, yon-der in the skies.

2. Seems that now I al-most see all the saint-ed dead, Ris-ing for that ju-bi-lee, that is just a-head; In the twink-ling of an eye, changed with them to be, All the liv-ing saints to fly to that ju-bi-lee.

3. When with all that heav'n-ly host we be-gin to sing, Sing-ing in the Ho-ly Ghost, how the heav'ns will ring; Mil-lions there will join the song, with them we shall be Prais-ing Christ thru a-ges long, heav-en's ju-bi-lee.

CHORUS

Oh, what sing-ing, Oh, what shout-ing,
What a day of sing-ing, sing-ing, what a day of shout-ing, shout-ing,
On that hap-py morn-ing when we all shall rise;
when we all shall glad-ly rise;

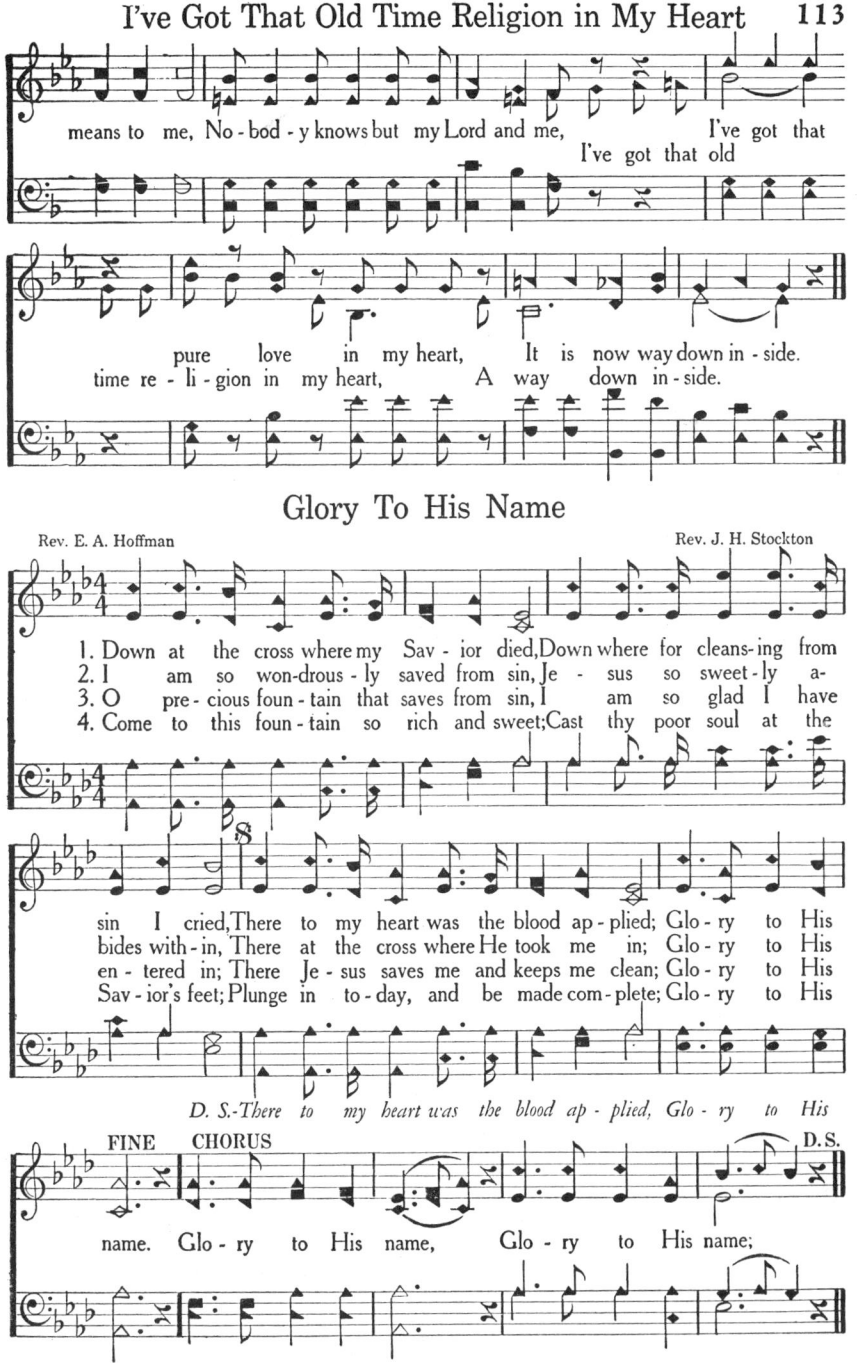

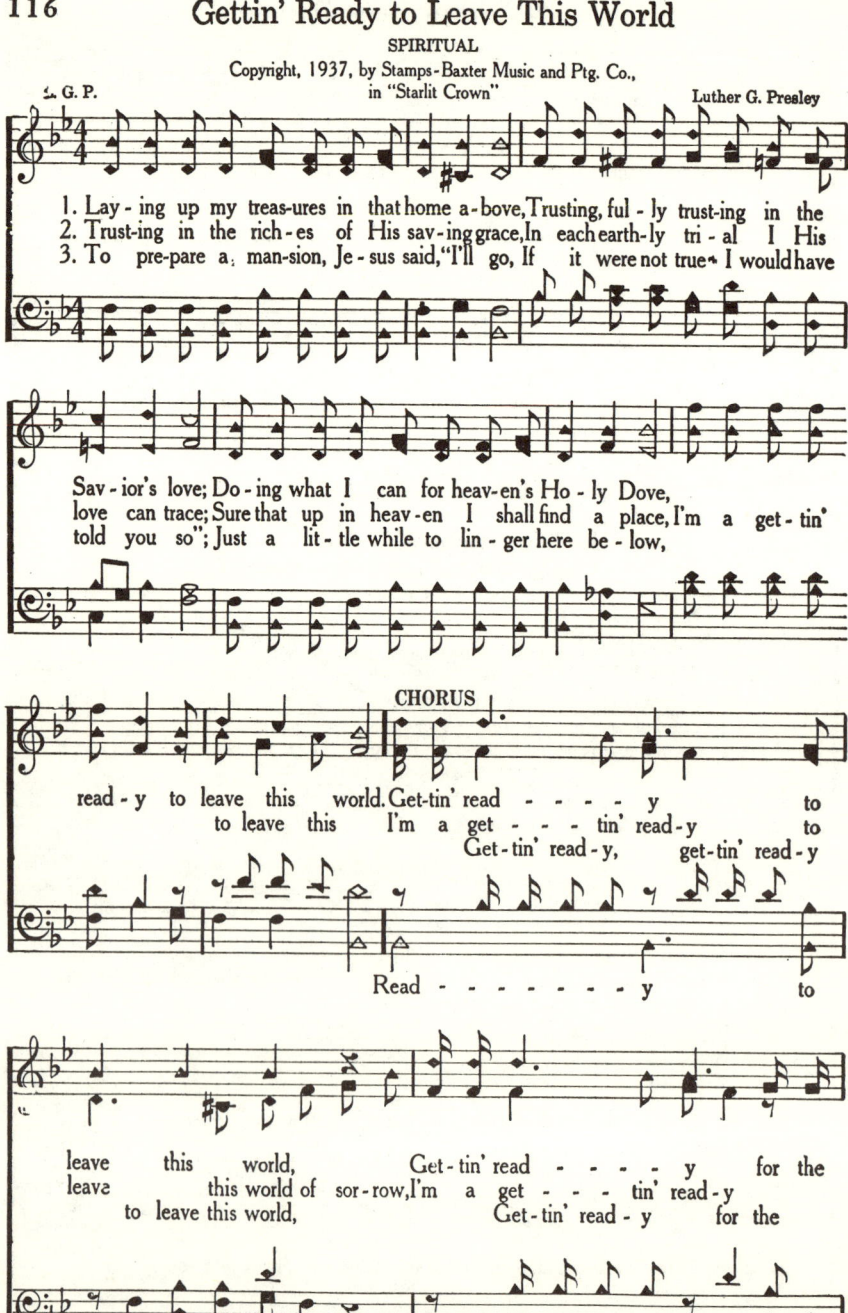

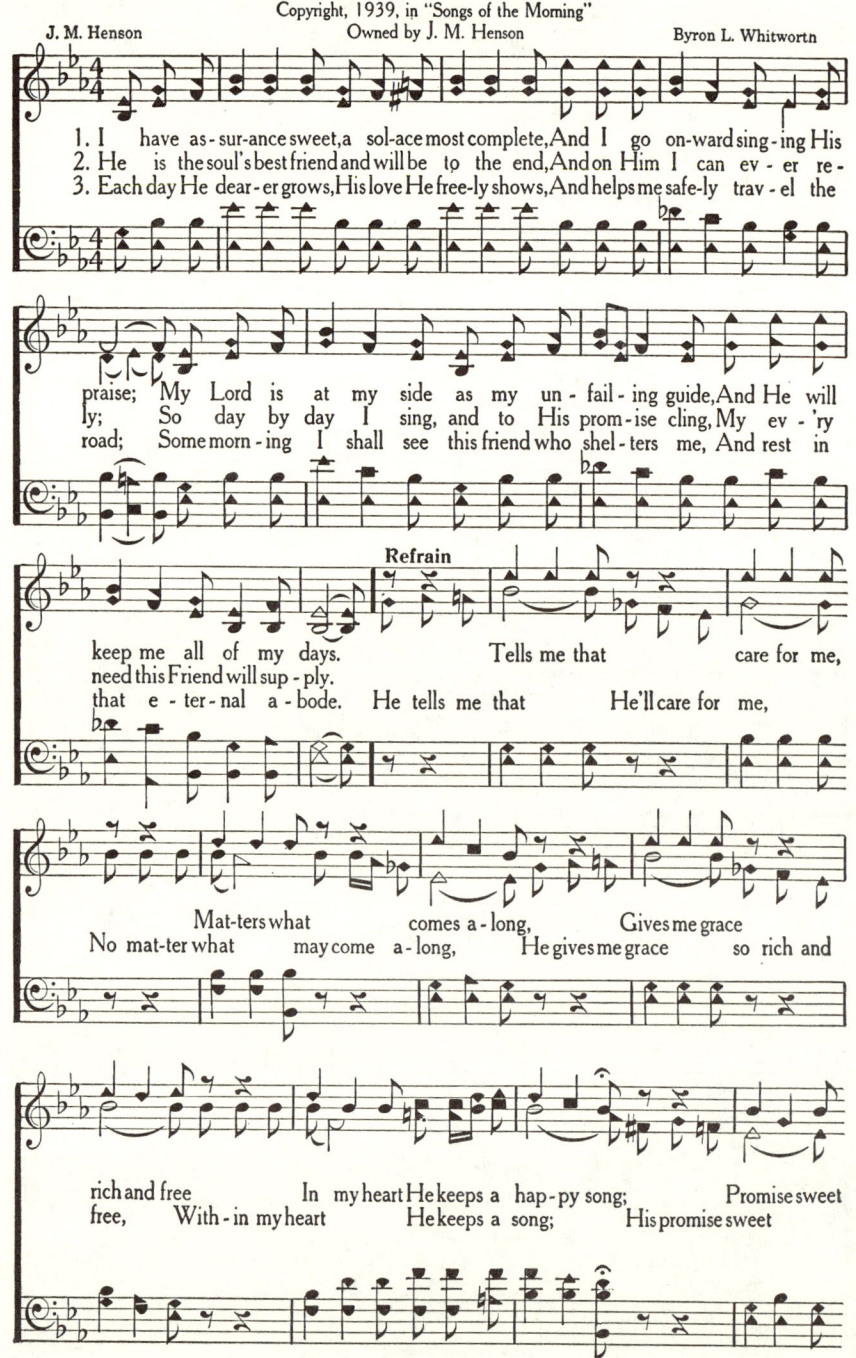

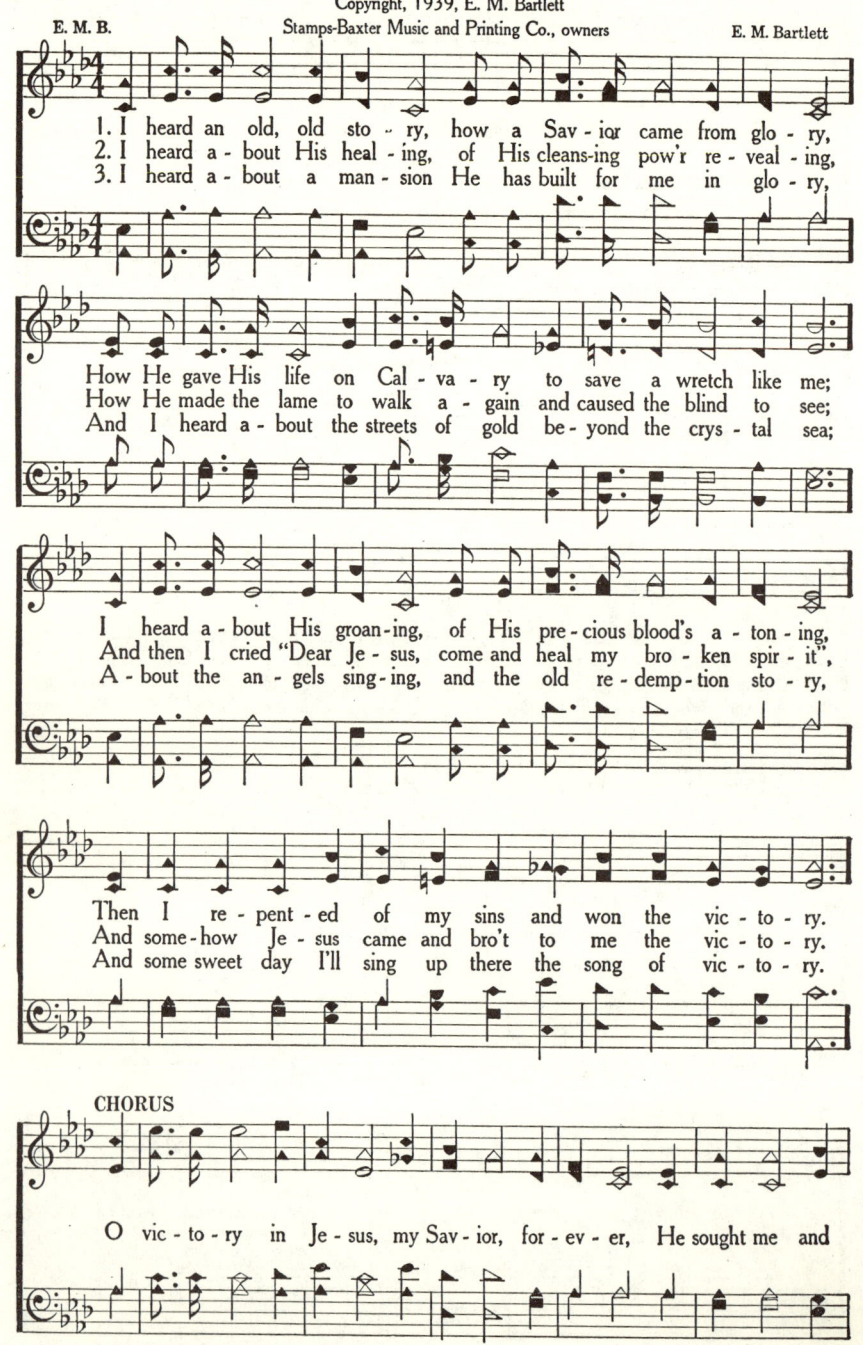

The Pearly White City

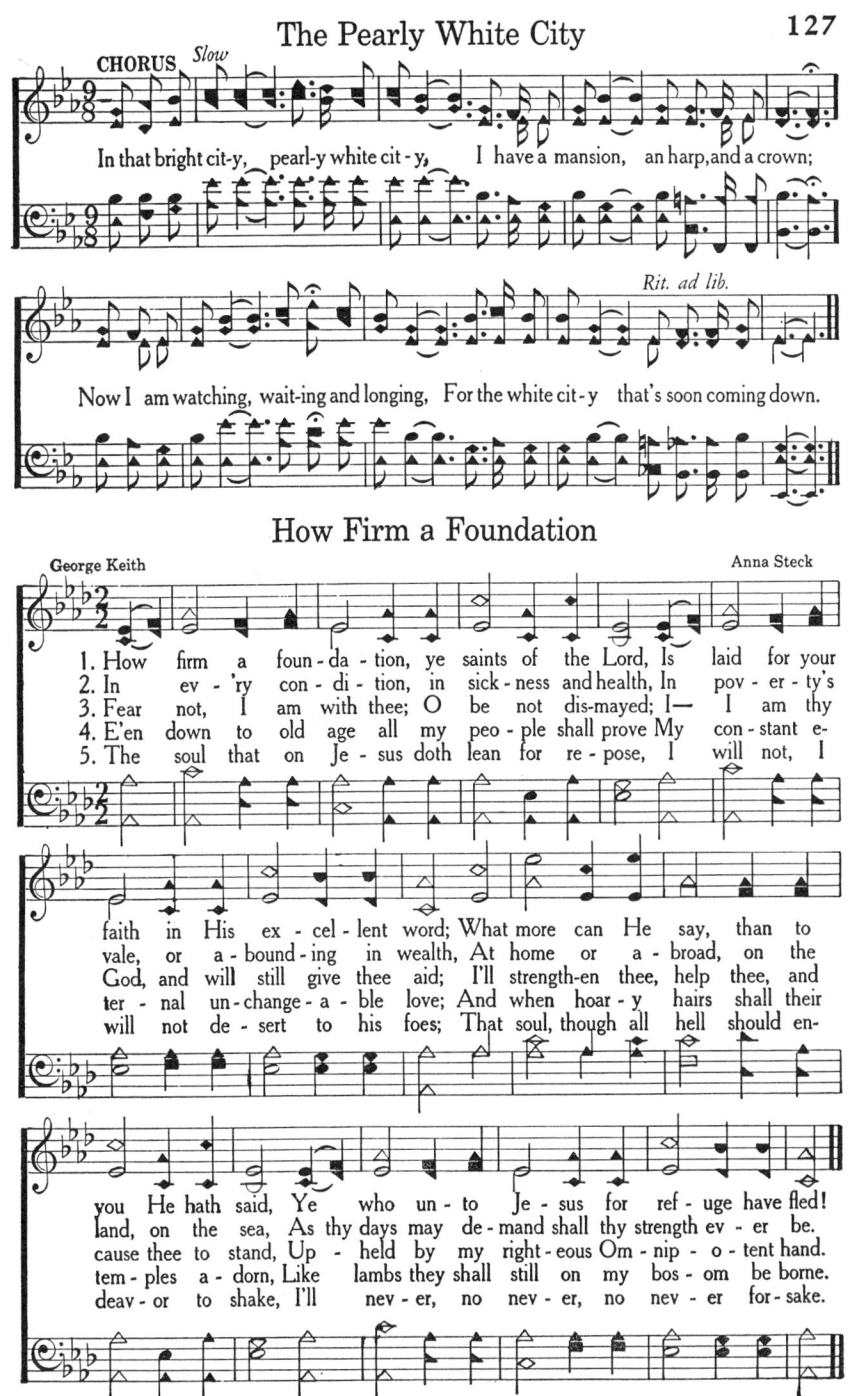

How Firm a Foundation

George Keith — Anna Steck

1. How firm a foundation, ye saints of the Lord, Is laid for your faith in His excellent word; What more can He say, than to you He hath said, Ye who unto Jesus for refuge have fled!
2. In ev'ry condition, in sickness and health, In poverty's vale, or abounding in wealth, At home or abroad, on the land, on the sea, As thy days may demand shall thy strength ever be.
3. Fear not, I am with thee; O be not dismayed; I— I am thy God, and will still give thee aid; I'll strengthen thee, help thee, and cause thee to stand, Upheld by my righteous Omnipotent hand.
4. E'en down to old age all my people shall prove My constant eternal unchangeable love; And when hoary hairs shall their temples adorn, Like lambs they shall still on my bosom be borne.
5. The soul that on Jesus doth lean for repose, I will not, I will not desert to his foes; That soul, though all hell should endeavor to shake, I'll never, no never, no never forsake.

I'll Meet You By the River

133

By the bright and shin-ing riv-er, Bright and shin-ing riv-er, so far a-way; far a-way;

D.S.

Aft-er we have flown these pris-on bars to a cit-y far be-yond the stars,

I Feel Like Traveling On

Wm. Hunter, D. D.   James D. Vaughan, owner.   Arr. by James D. Vaughan

With feeling.

1. My heav'nly home is bright and fair, I feel like trav-el-ing on, Nor pain, nor death can en-ter there, I feel like trav-el-ing on.
2. Its glit-t'ring tow'rs the sun out-shine, I feel like trav-el-ing on, That heav'n-ly man-sion shall be mine, I feel like trav-el-ing on.
3. Let oth-ers seek a home be-low, I feel like trav-el-ing on, Which flames de-vour, or waves o'er-flow, I feel like trav-el-ing on.
4. The Lord has been so good to me, I feel like trav-el-ing on, Un-til that bless-ed home I see, I feel like trav-el-ing on.

D. S.- My heav'n-ly home is bright and fair, I feel like trav-el-ing on.

FINE CHORUS

Yes, I feel like trav-el-ing on, I feel like trav-el-ing on;

D.S.

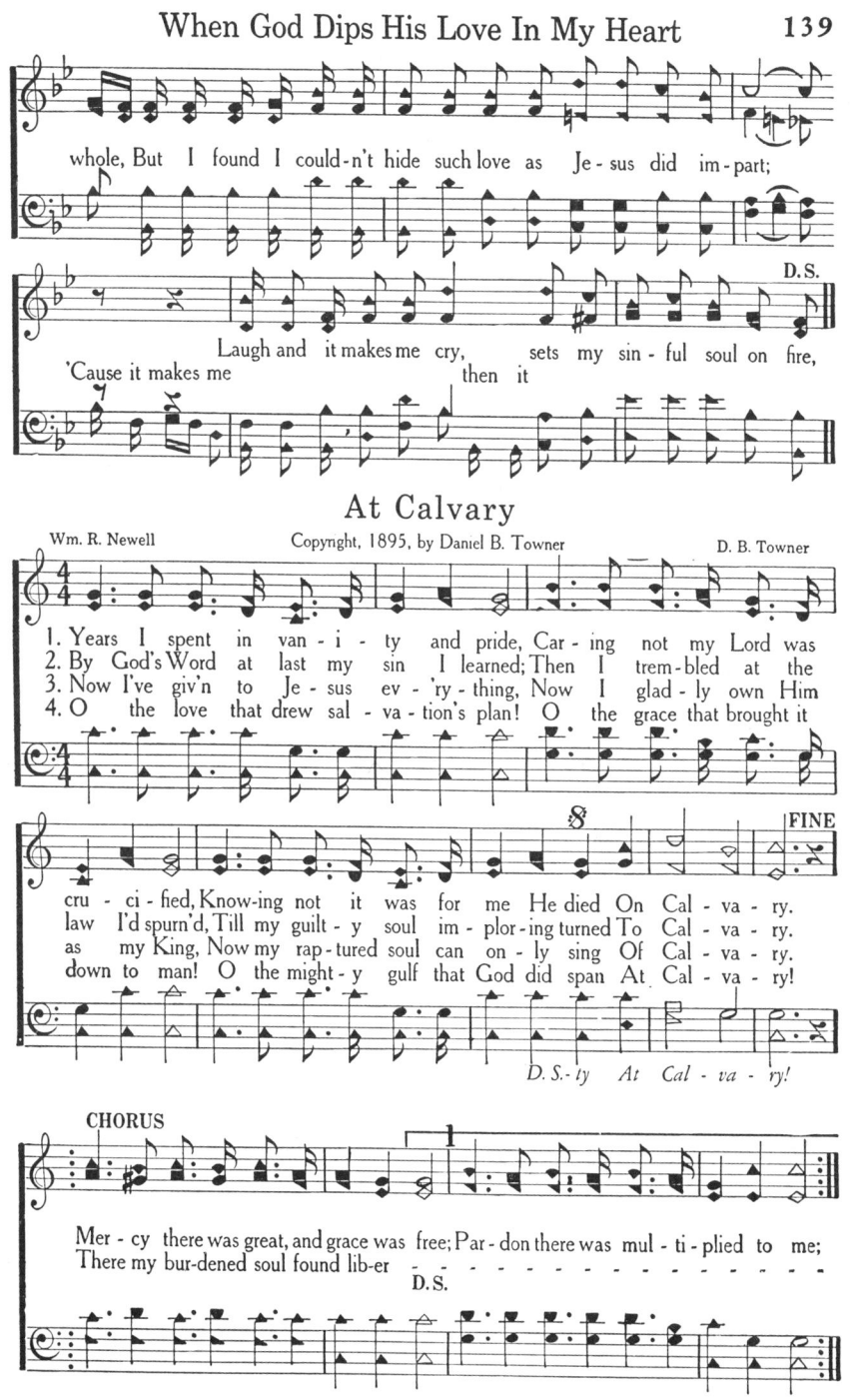

146. Press Along, Weary Pilgrim, Press On

Copyright, 1943, by Stamps-Baxter Music and Printing Co., in "Heaven's Lamp"

A. E. B. — Slow
Albert E. Brumley

1. Press a-long, wea-ry pil-grim, thru the strug-gles and strife, To that beau-ti-ful cit-y be-yond; Thru the paths of dis-ap-pointment, thru the cares of this life, Press a-long, wea-ry pil-grim, press on.
2. Press a-long, wea-ry pil-grim, tho' the path-way be dim, Soon the sor-rows of life will be done; Je-sus lead-eth like a shepherd, put your whole faith in Him, Press a-long, wea-ry pil-grim, press on.
3. Press a-long, wea-ry pil-grim, to the home of the soul, Where no part-ings or sorrow shall come; Where we'll all know one an-oth-er, and shall nev-er grow old, Press a-long, wea-ry pil-grim, press on.

CHORUS

Press a-long, wea-ry pil-grim, Press a-long, wea-ry pil-grim, Press a-long thru the shad-ows of night, Press thru shad-ows of night, Look a-bove to the por-tals, Look a-bove to the por-tals, Ev-er praying, ev-er sing-ing a song, Ev-er sing-ing a song, Press a-long, wea-ry pil-grim, press a-long wea-ry pil-grim, To that Press a-long wea-ry pil-grim, press a-long wea-ry pil-grim, Press a-

Press Along, Weary Pilgrim, Press On

Press Along to Glory-Land

James Rowe — Emmett S. Dean

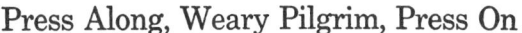

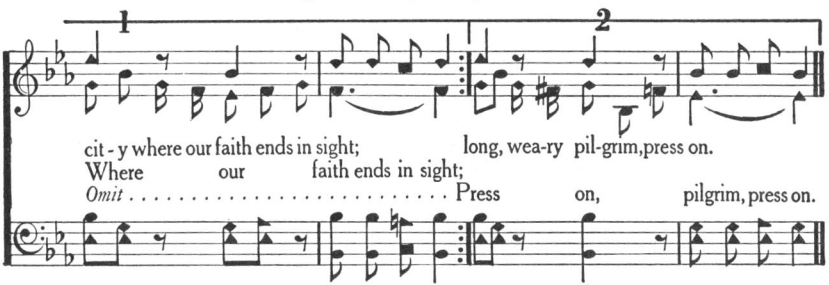

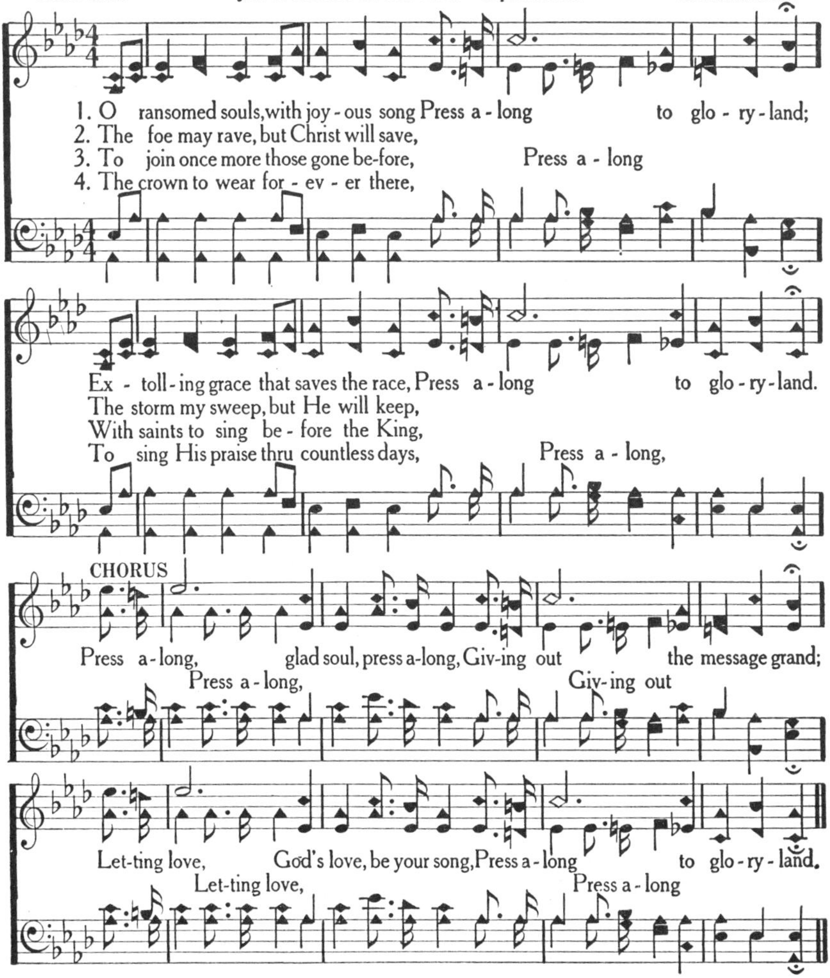

158 The Son Hath Made Me Free

Mirian E. Oatman Copyright, 1905, by W. A. Stewart R. E. Winsett, owner W. A. Stewart

1. I was once in E-gypt's bond-age (E-gypt's bond-age), But de-liv-'rance came to me (came to me); And I'm liv-ing now in Ca-naan (now in Ca-naan), For the Son hath made me free.
2. I was once a slave to Sa-tan (slave to Sa-tan), And he worked his will in me (yes, in me); But I'm bound by sin no long-er (bound no long-er),
3. Ere I en-tered in-to Ca-naan (in-to Ca-naan), In-bred sin re-mained in me (yes, in me); But from it I've found a cleansing (found a cleans-ing),
4. All my fear, all con-dem-na-tion (con-dem-na-tion), All that stood 'twixt God and me (God and me); Praise His name! are left be-hind me (left be-hind me), made me free.

CHORUS

I am dwell-ing now in Ca-naan, now in Ca-naan,
I am dwell-ing now in Ca-naan, Je-sus'
blood a-vails for me, yes, for me; I am free from con-dem-
blood a-vails for me; I am free from con-dem-

The Son Hath Made Me Free

na - tion, con-dem-na-tion, For the Son hath made me free.
na - tion, For the Son hath made me free.

I Am Praying for You

S. Cluff — Ira D. Sankey

1. I have a Sav - ior, He's plead - ing in glo - ry, A dear, lov - ing
2. I have a Fa - ther, to me He has giv - en A hope for e -
3. I have a robe, 'tis re-splend - ent in white-ness, A - wait - ing in
4. When Je - sus saves you, tell oth - ers the sto - ry, That my lov - ing

Sav - ior, tho' earth-friends be few; And now He is watch-ing in ten - der-ness
ter - ni - ty, bless - ed and true; And soon will He call me to meet Him in
glo - ry my won-der - ing view; O, when I re-ceive it all shin - ing in
Sav - ior is your Sav - ior too; Then pray that your Sav - ior may bring them to

CHORUS

o'er me, And O that my Sav - ior were your Sav - ior too.
heav - en, But O that He'd let me bring you with me too! For you I am
brightness, Dear friends, could I see you re - ceiv - ing one too!
glo - ry, And prayer will be answered, 'twas an-swered for you!

pray-ing, For you I am pray-ing, For you I am pray-ing, I'm pray - ing for you.

Mansions In Heaven

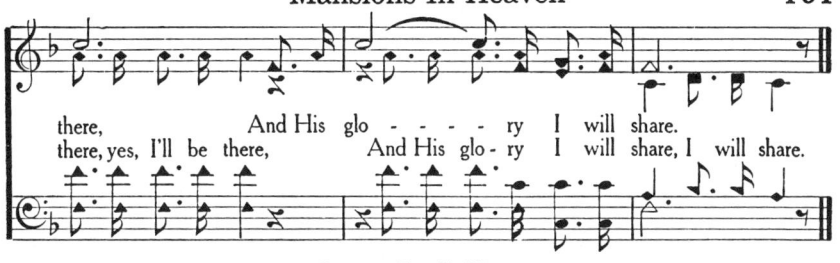

there, And His glo - - - - ry I will share.
there, yes, I'll be there, And His glo - ry I will share, I will share.

Jesus Is Calling

Fanny J. Crosby — Copyright, 1911, by Geo. C. Stebbins Renewal — George C. Stebbins

1. Je - sus is ten - der - ly call - ing thee home—Call-ing to - day, call - ing to - day;
2. Je - sus is call - ing the wea - ry to rest—Call-ing to - day, call - ing to - day;
3. Je - sus is wait - ing, O come to Him now—Waiting to - day, wait-ing to - day;
4. Je - sus is plead - ing, O list to His voice—Hear Him to - day, hear Him to - day;

Why from the sun-shine of love wilt thou roam Far - ther and far - ther a - way?
Bring Him thy bur - den, and thou shalt be blest; He will not turn thee a - way.
Come with thy sins, at His feet low - ly bow; Come, and no long - er de - lay.
They who be - lieve on His name shall re - joice; Quick - ly a - rise and a - way.

CHORUS

Call - - - ing to - day! Call - - - ing to - day!
Call - ing, call - ing to - day, to - day! Call - ing, call - ing to - day, to - day!

Je - - - - sus is call - - - ing, is ten - der - ly call - ing to - day.
Je - sus is ten - der - ly call - ing to - day,

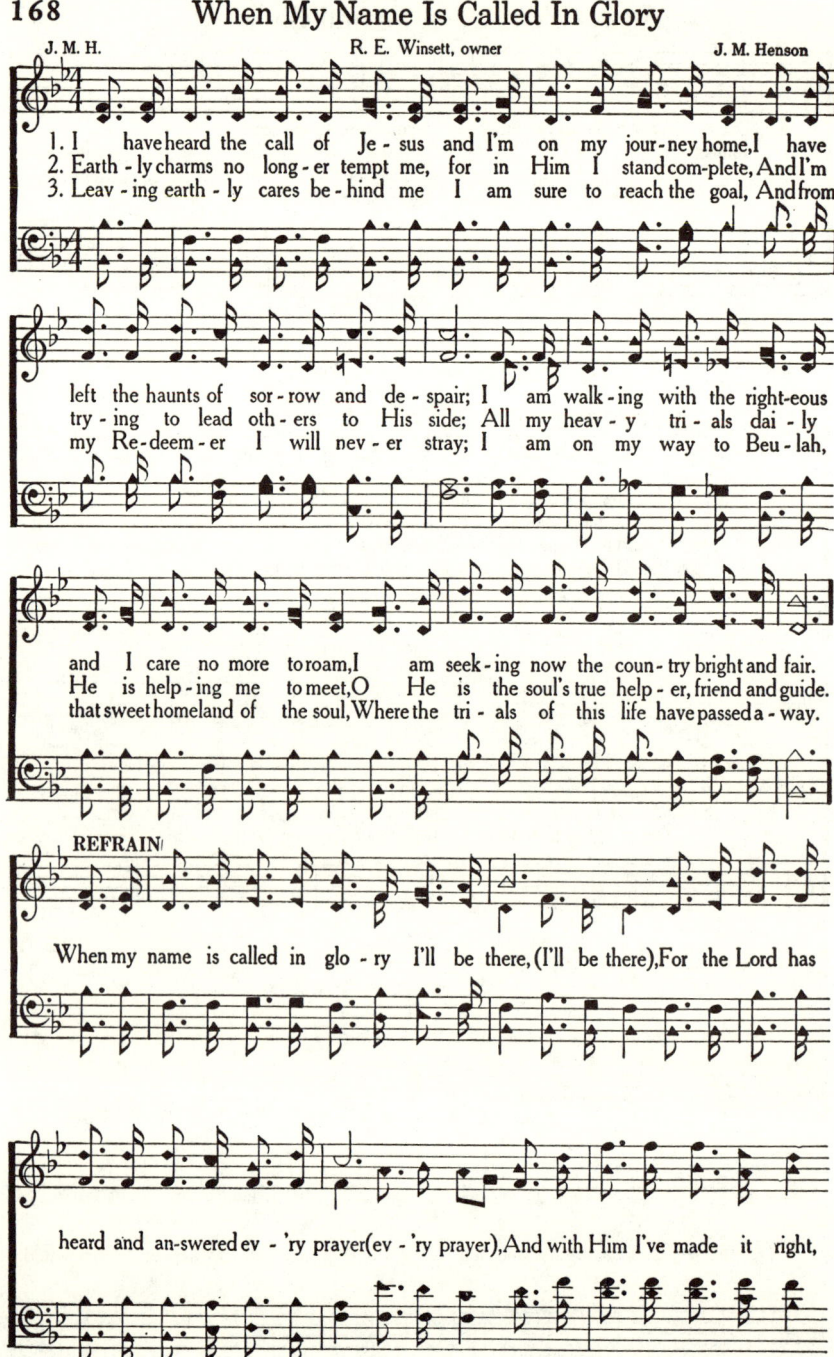

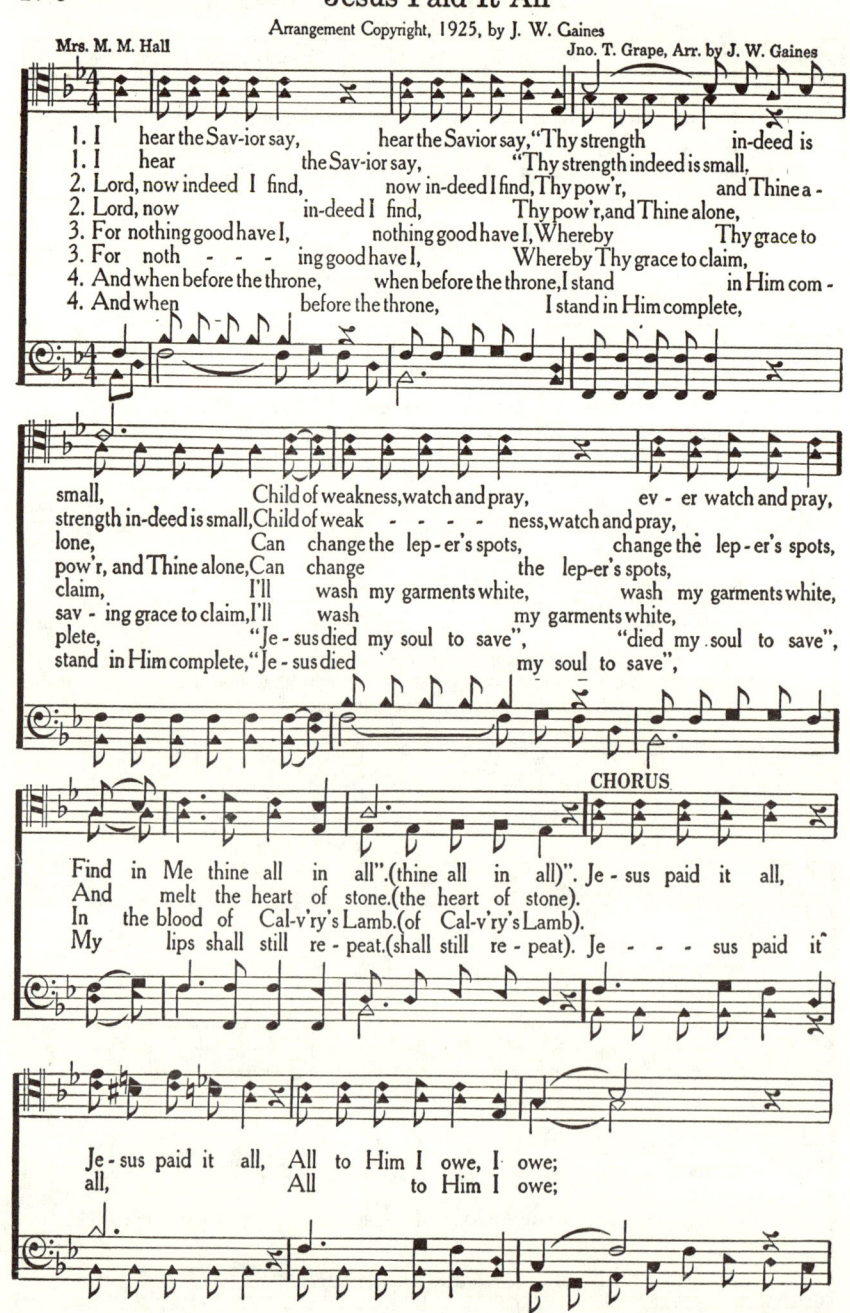

It Is Love — 173

sing its prais-es   While the hap - - - py a - ges roll.
sing its prais-es   While the hap-py a - ges roll, for-ev-er roll.

I Will Never Turn Back

"My Sheep hear my voice, and I know them, and they follow me" (Jesus) - John 10: 27
This little hymn is free to all publishers who will use it for the glory of God and His Son, our
R. N. G. 4th. verse R. E. W.   Savior. - J. E. T. and R. N. G.   R. N. Grisham

1. Once I wan-dered in dark-ness unsaved, Till the Sav-ior came knocking at my heart,
2. Of His love I will sing ev - 'ry day, Yes, I'll sing of His wondrous pow'r to save,
3. In His serv-ice each day may I be, Leading sin-ners to Je - sus to be healed,
4. Heal-ing bod - y and soul by His blood, And He keeps me each mo-ment by His pow'r,

And I o-pened the door, let Him in, Now rich bless-ings to me He im-parts.
For my Sav-ior is lead-ing the way, To those man-sions of glo-ry a - bove.
Thro' the blood flow-ing from Cal - va - ry, Till the light of His love is re-vealed.
I will walk in the light of His word, And be read-y to go an - y hour.

REFRAIN

I will nev - - - er turn back,   He's my light   ev - 'ry day;
Nev-er turn back,   nev - er turn back,   He is my light ev - 'ry hour and day;

No, I'll nev - - - er turn back,   For my Sav-ior is lead-ing the way.
Nev-er turn back,   nev - er turn back,

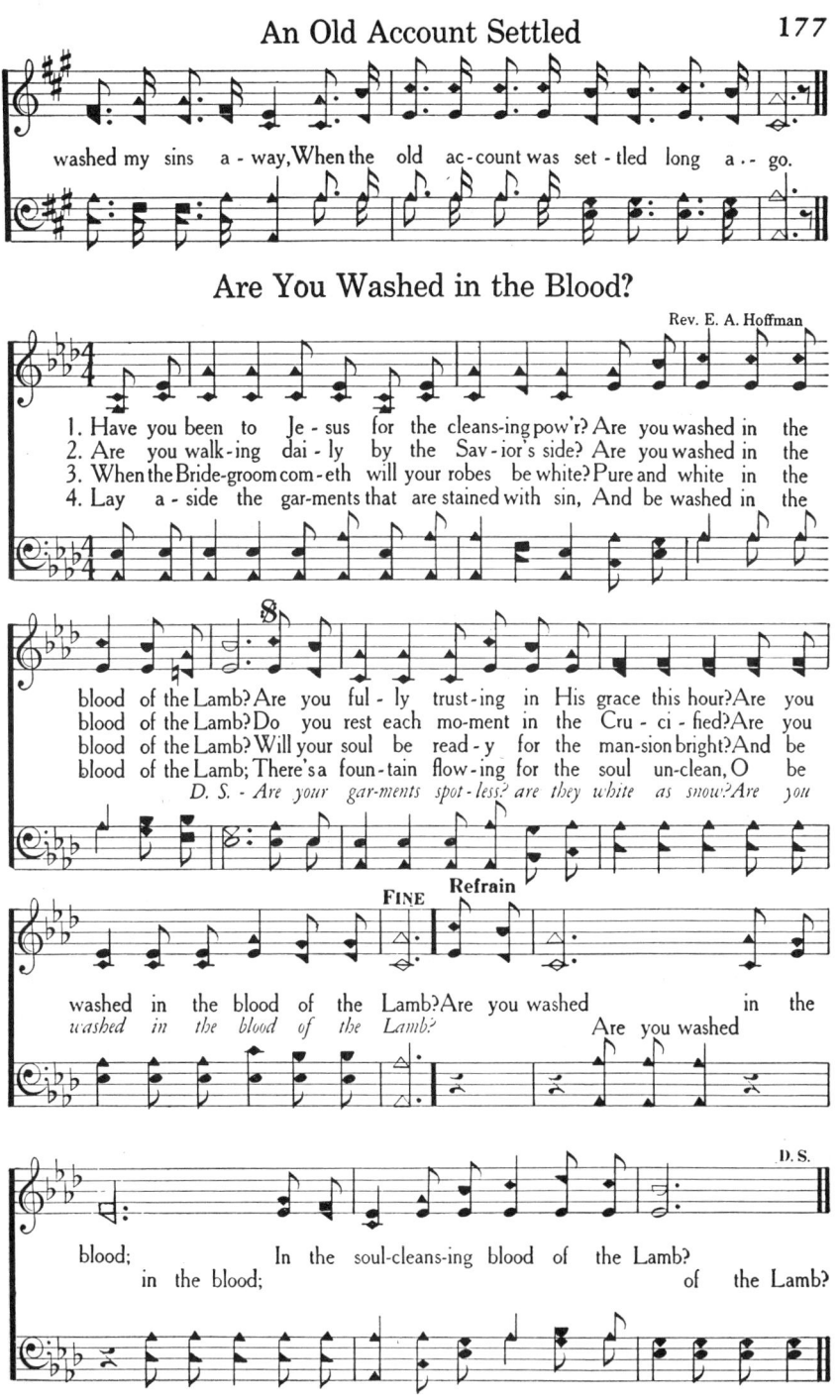

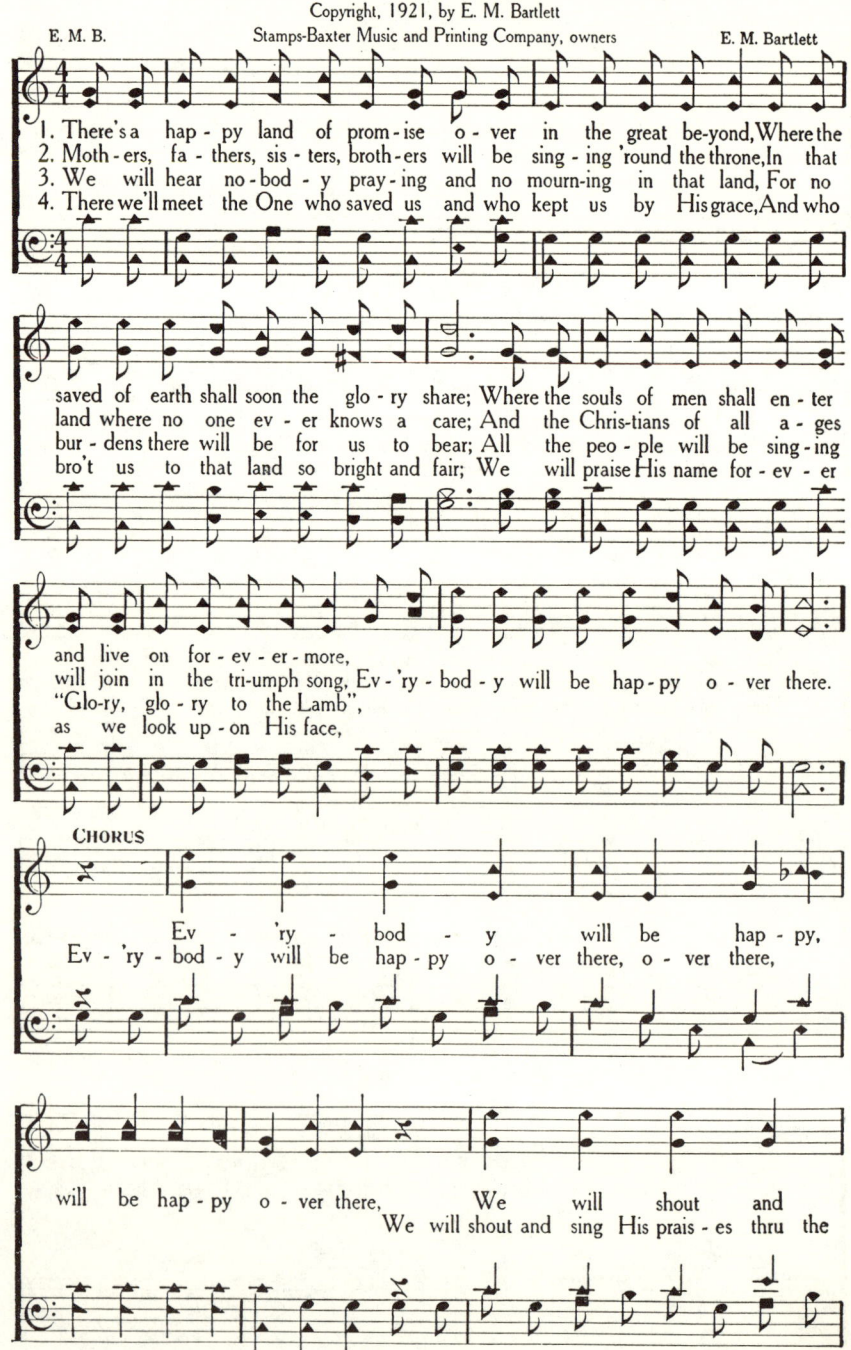

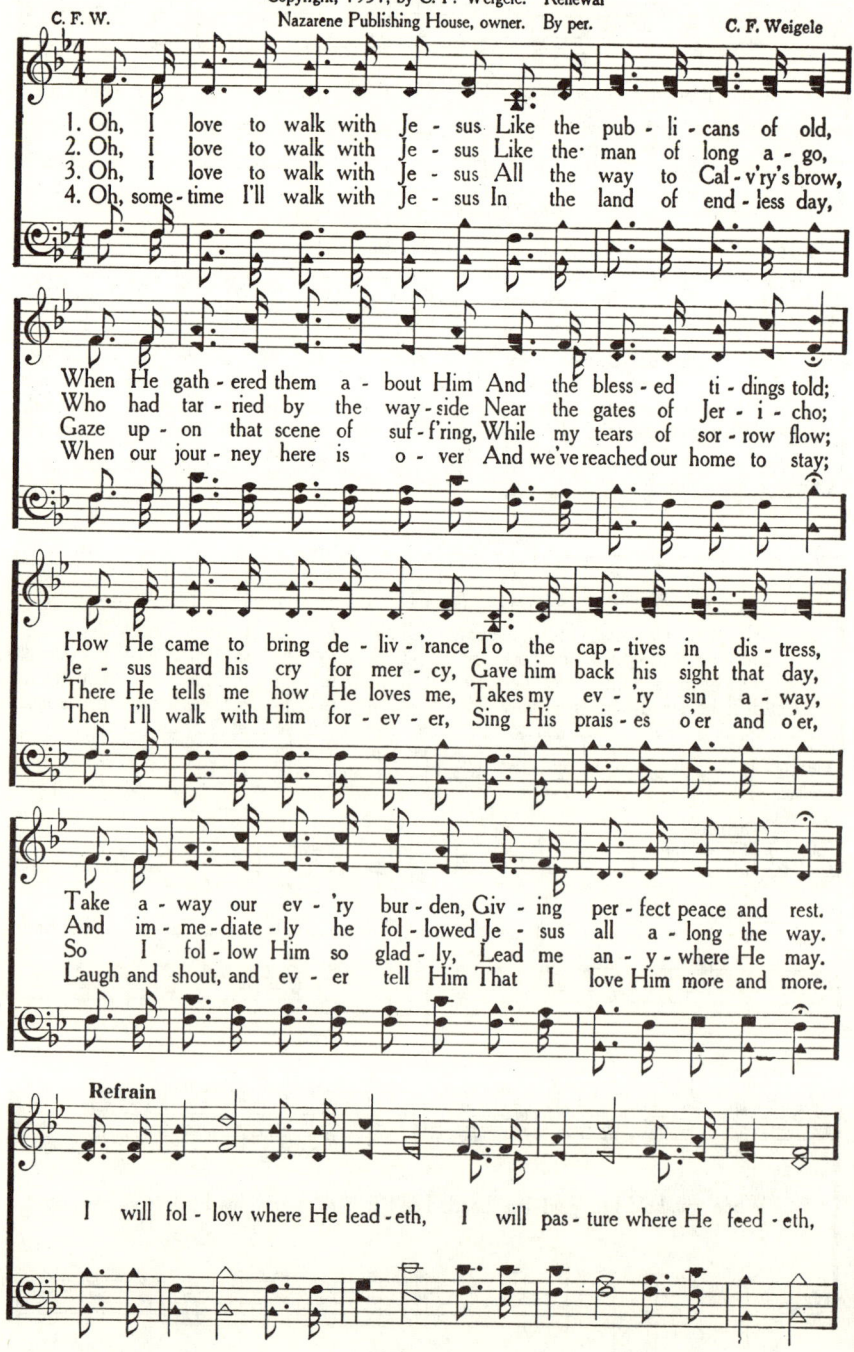

His Love

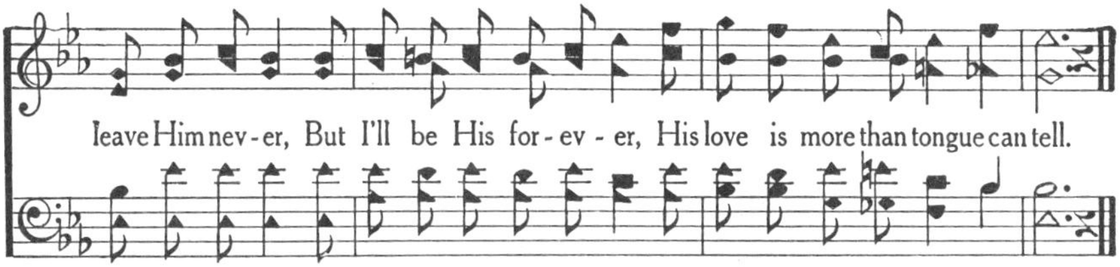

193

leave Him nev-er, But I'll be His for-ev-er, His love is more than tongue can tell.

Hide Me, Rock of Ages

Copyright, 1946, by O. A. Parris, in "Charming Refuge"
Assigned, 1947, to Stamps Quartet Music Co., Inc.

B. C. G.   Brantley C. George

1. O Thou bless-ed Rock of A-ges, (Rock of A-ges, I am) Trust-ing
2. Keep me when the storm-clouds gath-er, (storm-clouds gath-er, keep me) Till the
3. When my jour-ney is com-plet-ed, (is com-plet-ed, Sav-ior), And there's

now dear Lord in Thee; (dear Lord in Thee I'm trust-ing) Keep me till my
sun comes shin-ing thru; (comes shin-ing thru the shad-ows) Keep me till my
no more work to do; (no work to do, O bless-ed) Sav-ior guide my

D. S. - see; Thy face I see, in glo-ry, When the storm a-

FINE

jour-ney's end-ed, (jour-ney's end-ed, Keep me) Till Thy bless-ed face I see.
work is o-ver, (work is o-ver, Keep me) Till I bid this world a-dieu.
wea-ry spir-it, (wea-ry spir-it, To that) Hap-py land be-yond the blue.

round me rag-es, round me rag-es, Bless-ed Rock of A-ges hide Thou me.

CHORUS   D.S.

Hide me, O blest Rock of A - - - ges,   Till Thy bless-ed face I
A - ges, Rock of A - ges, hide me,

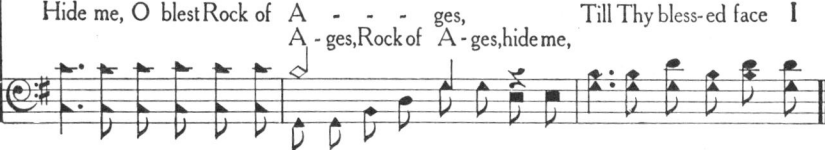

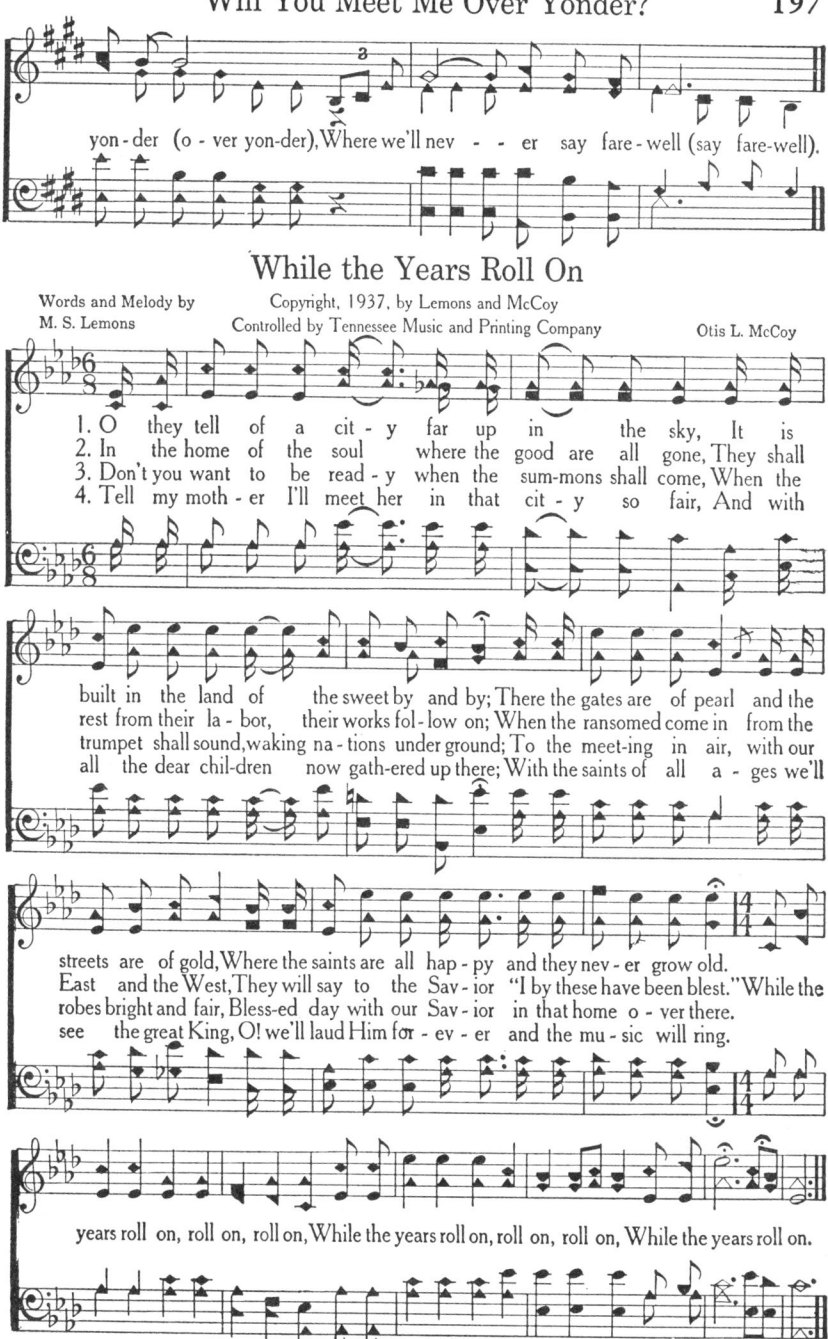

Whispering Hope

199

Mak - - - ing my heart in its sor - row re - joice.
Mak-ing my heart, mak-ing my heart in its sor - row re - joice.

Where the Soul Never Dies

Wm. M. G.   Copyright, 1942, Renewal. R. E. Winsett, owner   Wm. M. Golden

1. To Ca-naan's land I'm on my way, Where the soul (of man) nev - er dies;
2. A rose is bloom-ing there for me, Where the soul (of man) nev - er dies;
3. A love-light beams a - cross the foam, Where the soul (of man) nev - er dies;
4. My life will end in death-less sleep, Where the soul (of man) nev - er dies;
5. I'm on my way to that fair land, Where the soul (of man) nev - er dies;

My dark-est night will turn to day, Where the soul (of man) nev - er dies.
And I will spend e - ter - ni - ty, Where the soul (of man) nev - er dies.
It shines to light the shores of home, Where the soul (of man) nev - er dies.
And ev - er - last - ing joys I'll reap, Where the soul (of man) nev - er dies.
Where there will be no part - ing hand, And the soul (of man) nev - er dies.

CHORUS

No sad fare - wells, no tear - - - dimmed eyes,
Dear friends, there'll be no sad fare - wells, There'll be no tear-dimmed eyes,

Where all is love, and the soul nev - er dies.
Where all is peace and joy and love, And the soul of man nev - er dies.

200 When Our Lord Shall Come Again

Rev. Johnson Oatman, Jr.
R. L. Ferguson

1. When up-on...... the clouds of heav-en, (clouds of heav-en), Christ shall come.... to earth a-gain, (to earth a-gain), Will the world.... be glad to see Him, (glad to see Him), When our Lord... shall come a-gain? (shall come a-gain)?
2. Will His com - - ing bring re-joic-ing? (bring re-joic-ing)? Or will it ..... bring tears and pain? (bring tears and pain)? Are you read - y to re-ceive Him, (to receive Him), When our Lord... shall come a - gain? (shall come a - gain)?
3. Will you join.. .... in la - men - ta - tion? (la - men - ta - tion)? Or the an - - gels' glad re-frain? (their glad re-frain)? Will you help.... His peo-ple crown Him, (help to crown Him), When our Lord... shall come a - gain? (shall come a - gain)?
4. Work and pray....... till Je - sus calls you, (Je - sus calls you), Help to gath - - er in the grain, (the gold-en grain), Then with joy.... you'll meet the Sav - ior, (meet the Sav-ior), When our Lord... shall come a - gain? (shall come a - gain)?

CHORUS

There'll be sing-ing, there'll be shout-ing, There'll be sor-row, there'll be pain; There'll be weeping, there'll be
There'll be sing-ing, there'll be shout-ing, shout-ing, shout-ing, There'll be sorrow, there'll be pain, heart-rending pain; There'll be weeping, there'll be

202. I'll Live In Glory

J. M. H.  J. M. Henson

1. I'd like to stay here long-er than man's al-lot-ted days And watch the fleet-ing chang-es of life's un-e-ven ways, But if my Sav-ior calls me to that sweet home on high, I'll live with Him for-ev-er

2. I want to be of serv-ice a-long this pil-grim way, And lead the lost to Je-sus as fer-vent-ly I pray; As day by day I trav-el I'll keep Him ev-er nigh, And live with Him for-ev-er in glo-ry by and by.

3. The end I know is near-ing, by faith I look a-way To yon-der home su-per-nal, the land of end-less day; I'll cling to Him for-ev-er, and look be-yond the sky, And spend the end-less a-ges

CHORUS

O yes, I'll live in glo-ry by and by, I'll tell and sing love's
     live in glo-ry by and by,

sto-ry there on high; There with my dear Re-deem-er no
 tell love's sto-ry there on high;   there no

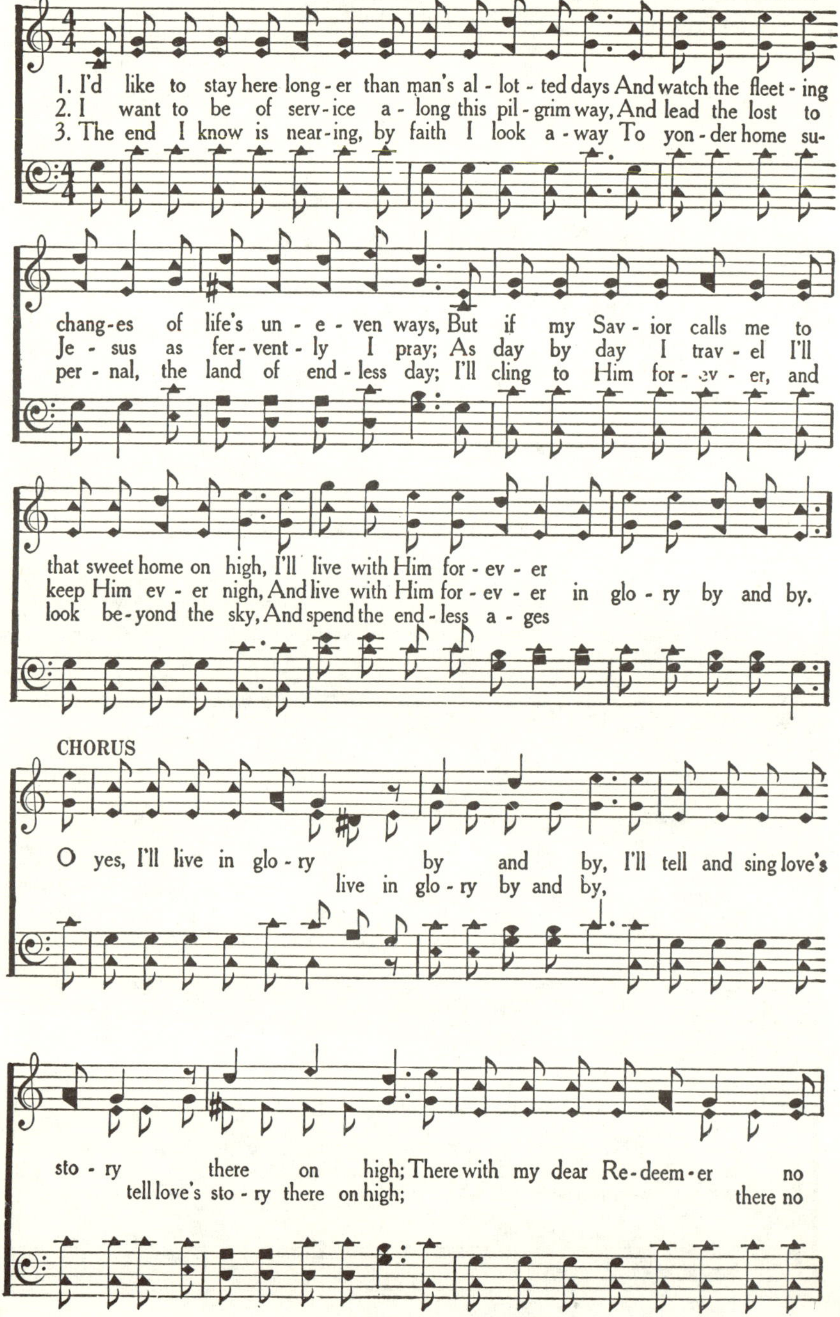

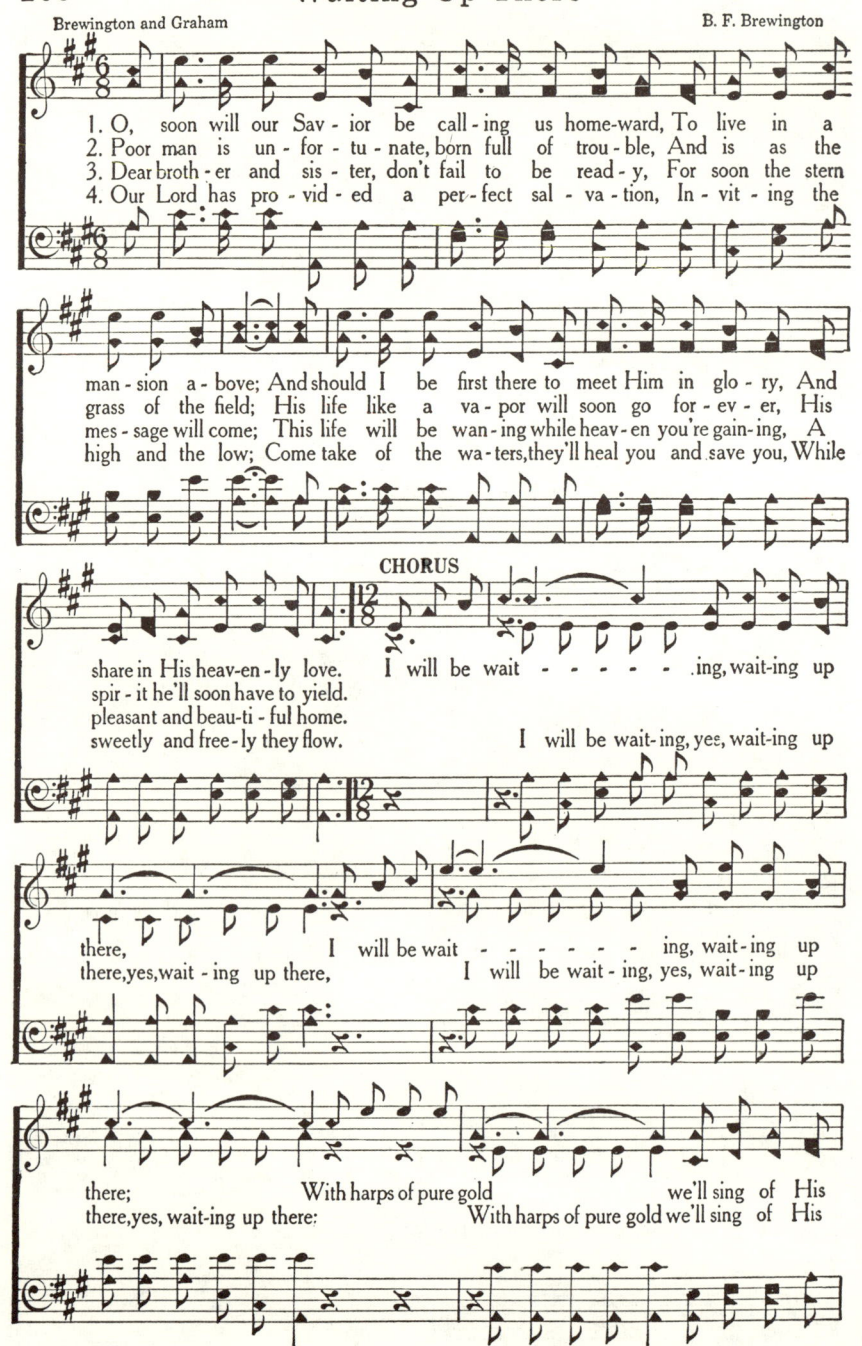

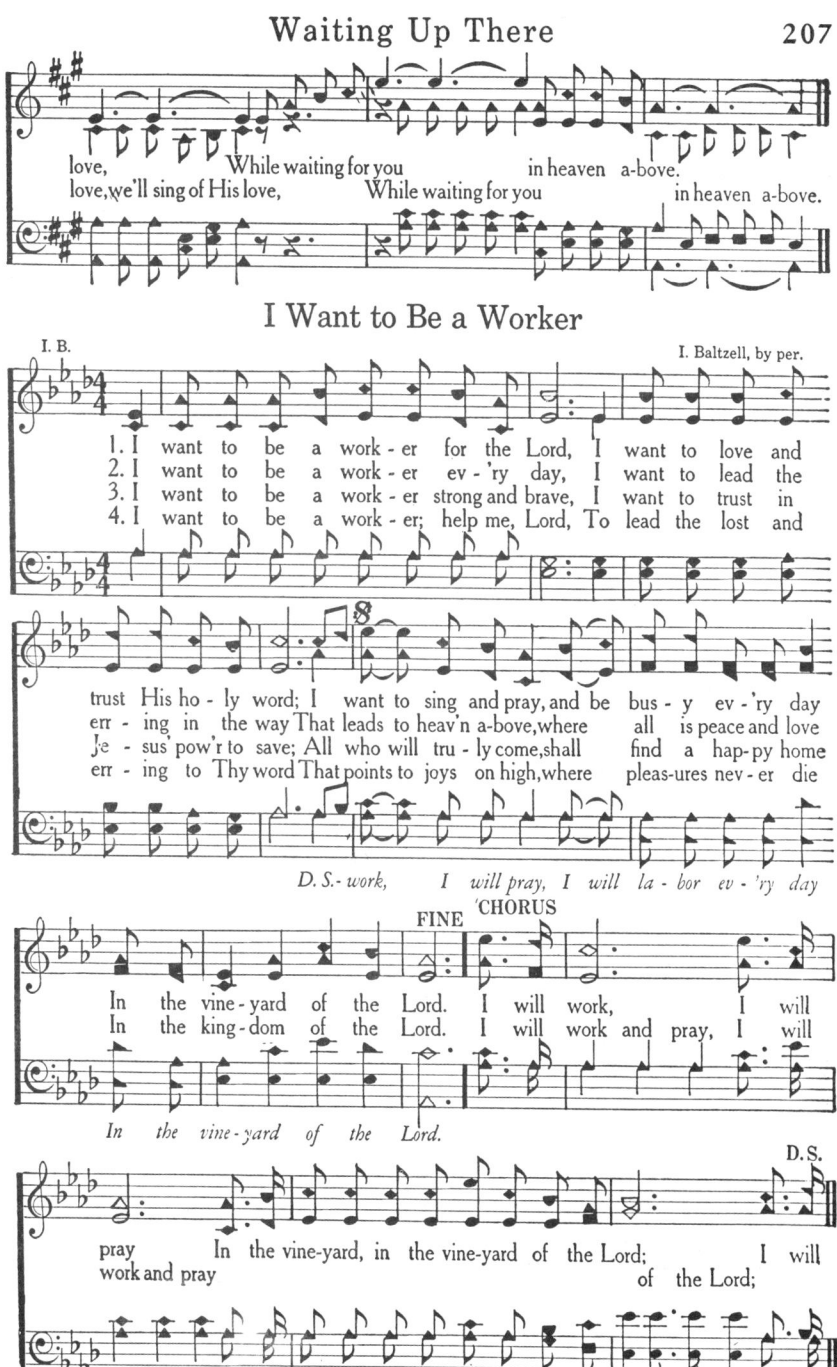

Echoes From the Glory Shore 211

sing-ing, sing-ing, hap-py an-gels sing-ing sweet Ech-oes from the glo-ry shore.
sing - - - ing, an-gels are sing-ing sweet

I'll Live On

T. J. L. Thos. J. Laney and V. C. Sparks, owners Thos. J. Laney

1. 'Tis a sweet and glo-rious tho't that comes to me, I'll live on, Yes, I'll live on;
2. When my bod-y's slumb'ring in the cold, cold clay,
3. When the world's on fire, and darkness veils the sun,
4. In the glo-ry land with Je-sus on the throne, I'll live on,

Je-sus saved my soul from death and now I'm free. I'll live on, yes, I'll live on,
There to sleep in Je-sus till the judgment day.
Men will cry and to the rocks and mountains run.
Thru e-ter-nal a-ges singing home sweet home. I'll live on,

CHORUS

I'll live on, yes, I'll live on, Thru e-ter-ni-ty I'll live on, and on,
on, on, on, on,

I'll live on, Yes, I'll live on, Thru e-ter-ni-ty I'll live on.
on, on, and on, yes, I'll live on.

Keep On The Firing Line

 Arr. Otis L. McCoy

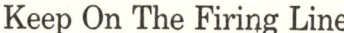

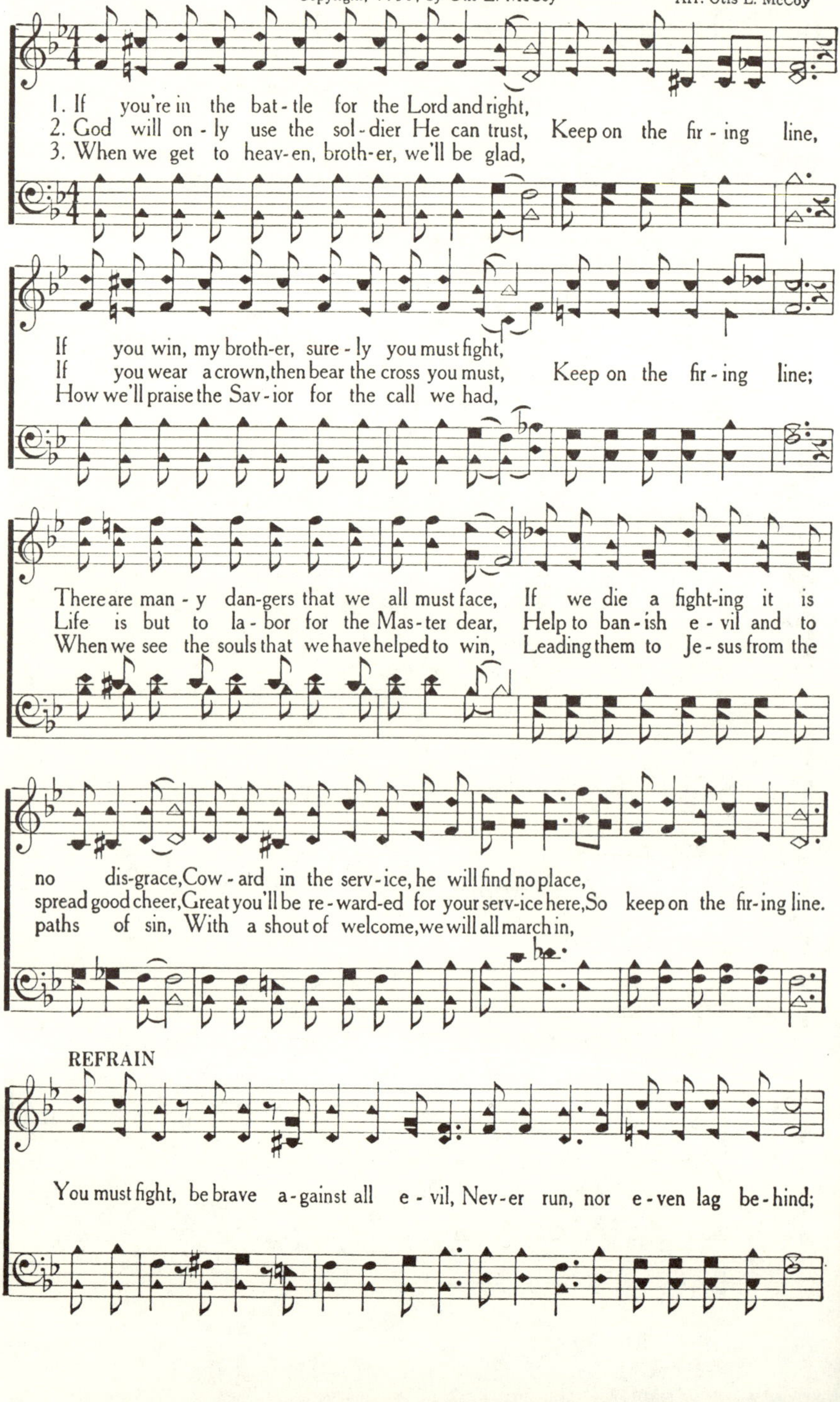

216. His Way With Thee

C. S. N.   Copyright, 1899, by H. L. Gilmour, Wenonah, N. J.   Rev. Cyrus S. Nusbaum

1. Would you live for Jesus and be always pure and good? Would you walk with Him within the narrow road? Would you have Him bear your burden, carry all your load? Let Him have His way with thee.
2. Would you have Him make you free, and follow at His call? Would you know the peace that comes by giving all? Would you have Him save you, so that you need never fall? Let Him have His way with thee.
3. Would you in His kingdom find a place of constant rest? Would you prove Him true in providential test? Would you in His service labor always at your best? Let Him have His way with thee.

CHORUS

His pow'r can make you what you ought to be; His blood can cleanse your heart and make you free; His love can fill your soul, and you will see 'Twas best for Him to have His way with thee.

When the Home Gates Swing Open

223

O. A. P.
James D. Vaughan, owner, 1927
O. A. Parris

1. I am on the up-ward road, lead-ing to that bright a-bode, Where for-ev-er my soul shall be free (be free); Won't that be a hap-py time, heav-en's bells will sweet-ly chime, When the home gates swing o-pen for me.

2. Tho' some-time the path may lead thru the vale of sin and greed, Je-sus ev-er my ref-uge will be (will be); Soon at home my tri-als o'er, I shall praise Him ev-er-more, and a crown of glo-ry wear, for me.

3. I'll keep walk-ing in His light, till my faith shall end in sight, He will lead me till safe o'er the sea (the sea); I shall find a wel-come there,

CHORUS

That will be a hap-py day, When the clouds have passed a-way; From my cares I shall be free,

That will be a hap-py day, When all the clouds have passed a-way; From my cares I shall be free,

That will be a hap-py day, When all the clouds have passed a-way; From my cares I shall be free,

Saved, Saved!

J. P. S J. P. Scholfield

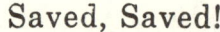

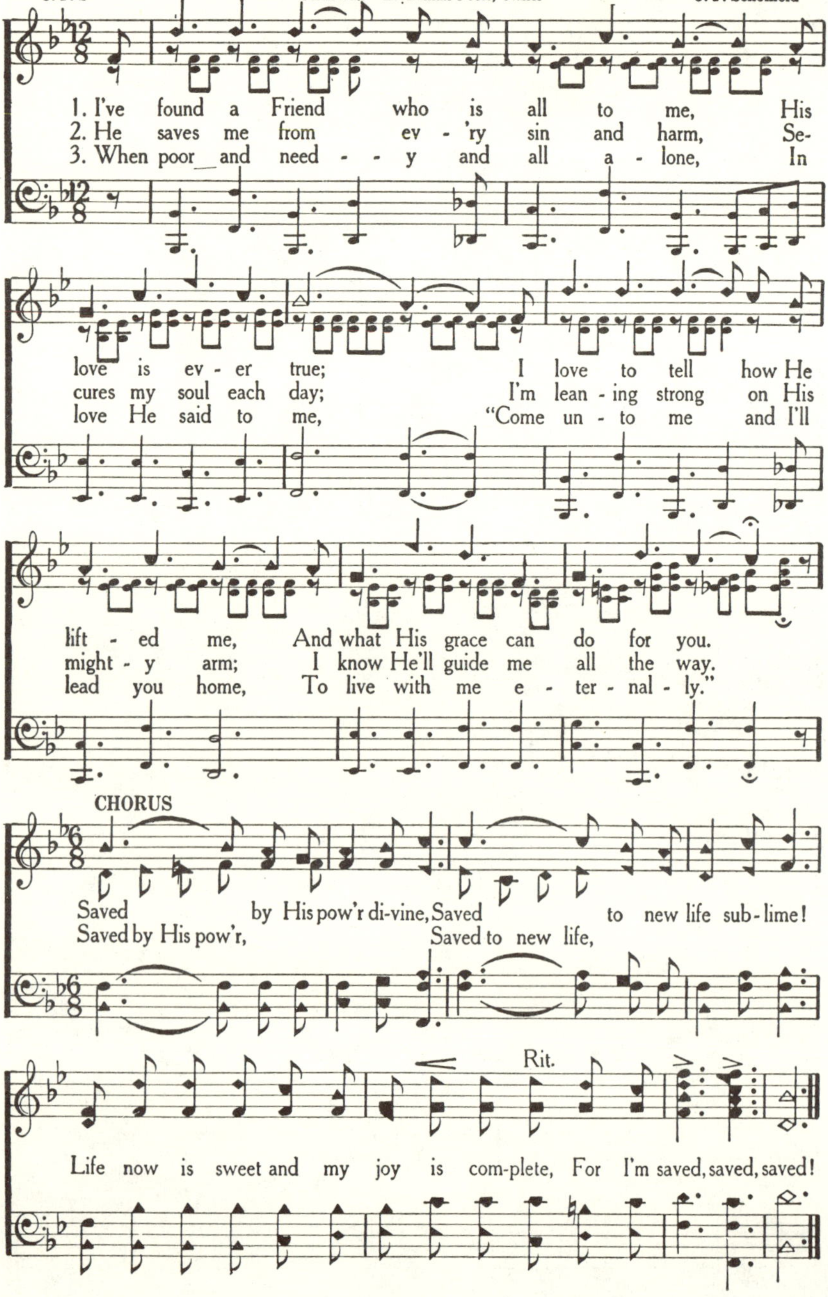

Glory Hallelujah in My Soul

G. T. B.
Copyright owned by R. E. Winsett
G. T. Byrd

1. When I came to Christ, I was all de-filed, Now there's glo-ry hal-le-
2. Yes, I came to Christ with my load of sin, There's a glo-ry hal-le-
3. Come, O wan-der-er, come and go with me, There's a glo-ry hal-le-
4. I will hon-or Christ where-so-e'er I go, There's a glo-ry hal-le-
5. When I leave the earth I will say good-by, There's a glo-ry hal-le-

lu-jah in my soul; Since I saw the blood and was rec-on-ciled,
lu-jah in my soul; And I plead and knock'd till He let me in,
lu-jah in my soul; Come and see what Christ's blood will do for thee,
lu-jah in my soul; His blood has washed me as white as snow,
lu-jah in my soul; I will soar t'ward heav'n, far a-bove the sky,

Refrain

There's a glo-ry hal-le-lu-jah in my soul. There is glo - - ry,
There is glo-ry,

there is glo - - ry, There's a glo-ry hal-le-lu-jah in my soul; There is
there is glo-ry,

glo - - ry, there is glo - - ry, There's a glo-ry hal-le-lu-jah in my soul.
There is glo-ry, there is glo-ry,

Battle Hymn

229

Rev. I. Watts, D. D.   English Arr. by Wm. B. Blake

1. Am I a soldier of the cross, A fol-l'wer of the Lamb, And shall I fear to own His cause, Or blush to speak His name?
2. Must I be carried to the skies On flow-'ry beds of ease, While others fought to win the prize, And sailed thru bloody seas?
3. Are there no foes for me to face, Must I not stem the flood? Is this vile world a friend to grace, To help me on to God?
4. Sure I must fight if I would reign, Increase my courage, Lord; I'll bear the toil, endure the pain, Supported by Thy Word.

CHORUS

And when the battle's over we shall wear a crown! Yes, we shall wear a crown! Yes, we shall wear a crown! And when the battle's over we shall wear a crown In the new Jerusalem.

D.S. — Wear a crown, wear a crown, Wear a bright and shining crown;
      Wear a crown, wear a crown,

Glory Is Coming

231

Copyright, 1926, in "Crowning Hymns" No. 6
H. F. Morris, owner

James Rowe — Pledger B. Jones

1. Liv-ing in His pres-ence and in true ac-cord, Dai-ly I am work-ing for my bless-ed Lord; Sure that He will give to me a rich re-ward And that glo-ry is com-ing soon.
2. Of-ten I am wea-ry and at times de-prest; Long-ing for the homeland and its joy and rest; But each day I'm near-er to that coun-try blest And my glo-ry is com-ing soon.
3. At the shin-ing por-tal He my soul will meet, With a word of wel-come and a smile so sweet; Then, O then with rap-ture I my Lord shall greet! Yes, my glo-ry is com-ing soon.

Refrain

Glo - ry's com-ing it won't be long! I'll be sing-ing the glad new song, I'll be faith-ful and brave and strong, Glo-ry's com-ing it won't be long.

Sure-ly it is com-ing it won't be long! I shall soon be sing-ing the hap-py, glad new song, Yes, I will be faith-ful, al-ways brave and faith-ful,

It is com-ing and it won't be long, it's com-ing, I'll be sing-ing heav-en's glad new song in glo-ry, Al-ways not long.

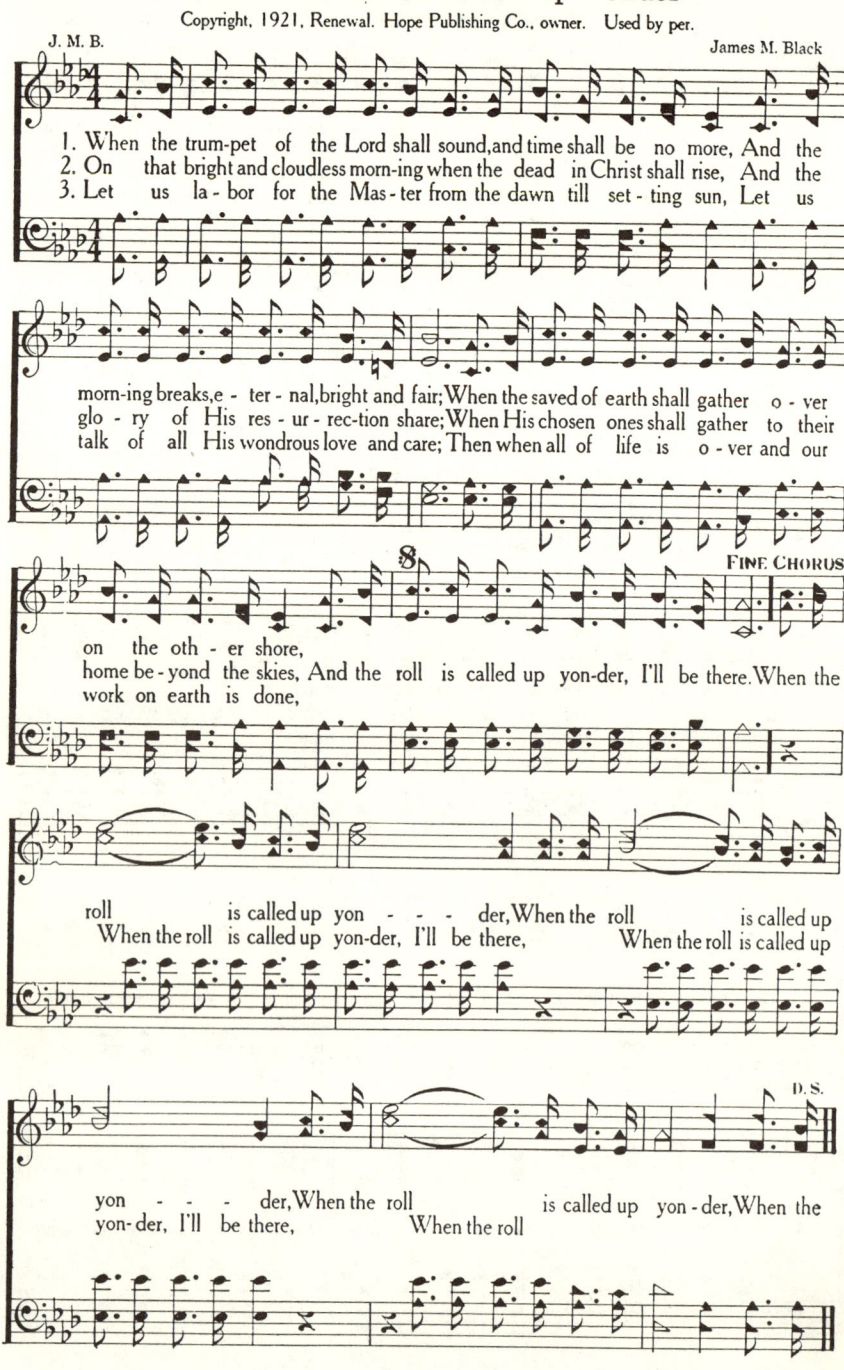

Just Because He Loved Me So

241

J. E. French

1. Come, hear me tell the story Paul and Silas loved so well, How Jesus left His home above and came on earth to dwell;
   You ask me why He suffered, I can only say "I know", He gave His life a ransom, just because He loved me so.
2. I'm glad my dear Redeemer walked beside the Galilee, His life was pure and holy, and His grace was full and free;
   He calls for me to follow, I will walk with Him below, He will never, never leave me, just because He loved me so.
3. I will sing His boundless mercy, all the beauty of His ways If at times I do not see Him, I will trust and give Him praise;
   And no matter where He leads me, it is best for me, I know, I will lean upon His promise, just because He loved me so.

CHORUS

He loved me so, He loved me so; He gave His life a ransom, Just because He loved me so; cause He loved me so.
He loved, He loved me so, He loved, He loved me so;

Jesus Keeps Me Happy

243

Claude P. Ganus — Owned by authors — L. H. Bradford

1. Won-der-ful is Je-sus whom I now a-dore, Ev-'ry day and hour I praise Him more and more; Mar-vel-ous the vi-sions that I see each day,
2. Tri-als may be-set me but I'll not re-pine, Grace to o-ver-come them al-ways will be mine; Giv-ing strength and cour-age, at my side He'll stay,
3. I shall share His glo-ry when I cease to roam, I shall praise Him ev-er in the soul's bright home; That I may be with Him thro' the end-less day,

FINE CHORUS

Je-sus keeps me hap-py in the glo-ry way. Je-sus keeps me hap-py, Keeps me

D.S.-Je-sus keeps me hap-py in the glo-ry way.

sing-ing all the time, More and more I praise Him As the hills of life I

D.S.

climb to glo-ry, He's my light and glad-ness, Ev-'ry mo-ment of the day,

Just Over the Stars

244
L. O.
Logan Oskin

Not too fast

1. There is a land of pure de-light, Where trou-ble nev-er mars;
2. Our Sav-iour there at last we'll meet, When we shall cross the bars,
3. We'll sing and shout with that glad throng, When safe from Sa-tan's wars;

But joy and peace for-ev-er reigns, 'Tis the land just o-ver the stars.
He'll bid us wel-come home up there, In that land just o-ver the stars.
And praise our Sav-iour ev-er-more, In that land just o-ver the stars.

CHORUS

Just o — — ver the stars, Just o — — ver the stars,
Just o-ver the beau-ti-ful shin-ing stars, Just o-ver the beau-ti-ful shin-ing stars,

1. The blood-washed throng will sing "Sweet home", In that land just o-ver the stars,

2. We soon shall stand with that an-gel band, In that land just o-ver the stars.

246. My Mother's Bible

M. B. Williams
Copyright, 1893, by Chas. D. Tillman
Charlie D. Tillman

1. There's a dear and precious Book, Tho' it's worn and faded now, Which recalls those happy days of long ago, When I stood at mother's knee, With her hand upon my brow, And I heard her voice in gentle tones and low.
2. As she read the stories o'er, Of those mighty men of old, Of Joseph and of Daniel and their trials, Of little David bold, Who became a king at last, Of Satan and His many wicked wiles.
3. Then she read of Jesus' love, As He blest the children dear, How He suffered, bled and died upon the tree; Of His heavy load of care, Then she dried my flowing tears, With her kisses as she said it was for me.
4. Well, those days are past and gone, But their mem'ry lingers on, And the dear old Book each day has been my guide; And I seek to do His will, As my mother taught me then, And ever in my heart His words abide.

FINE

D. S.—As I walk the narrow way That leads at last to that bright home above.

CHORUS

Bless-ed Book, precious Book, On thy dear old tear-stained
Bless-ed Book, precious Book,

D. S.

leaves I love to look; (love to look); Thou art sweeter ev'ry day,

248 Just Over in the Glory-Land

Jas. W. Acuff
Copyright, 1906, by Dean and Acuff
Emmett S. Dean

1. I've a home prepared where the saints abide, Just over in the glory-land;
And I long to be by my Savior's side, Just over in the glory-land.

2. I am on my way to those mansions fair, Just over in the glory-land;
There to sing God's praise and His glory share, Just over in the glory-land.

3. What a joyful tho't, that my Lord I'll see, Just over in the glory-land;
And with kindred saved, there forever be, Just over in the glory-land.

4. With the blood-washed throng I will shout and sing, Just over in the glory-land;
Glad hosannas to Christ, the Lord and King, Just over in the glory-land.

REFRAIN

Just o— — —ver in the glory-land, I'll join the happy angel band,
Just o-ver, o-ver in the glory-land, I'll join, yes, join the happy angel band,
Just o-ver in the glory-land; Just o— — —ver in the glory land, There
 Just o-ver, o-ver in the glory land,
with the mighty host I'll stand, Just over in the glory-land.
with, yes, with the mighty host I'll stand,

In the Great Triumphant Morning

261

R. E. W.
Owned by R. E. Winsett, Dayton, Tenn.
R. E. Winsett

1. In the great tri-um-phant morn-ing, when we hear the Bridegroom cry, And the dead in Christ shall rise,
2. In the great tri-um-phant morn-ing, what a hap-py time 'twill be, When the Lord de-scends in glo-ry,
3. In the great tri-um-phant morn-ing, when the har-vest is complete, And the ransomed dead, they all shall rise,
4. In the great tri-um-phant morn-ing, all the king-doms we'll pos-sess, Then the

1. We'll be changed to life im-mor-tal, In the twink-ling of an eye, And meet Je - - - - - sus in the skies, up in the skies,(heav'n-ly skies).
2. Sets His wait-ing chil-dren free, And we meet Him in the glo-ry,
3. Reign as kings and priests e-ter-nal, Christ and all the loved ones meet, In the rap - - - - - ture in the mor-tal,
4. We'll be crowned with life im-mor-tal, Un-der Christ for-ev-er blest, Aft-er meet - - - - - ing in the

And meet Je-sus in the skies, up in the skies,(heav'n-ly skies).

REFRAIN

We shall all rise to meet Him, we shall all go to greet Him,

1. In the morning when the dead in Christ shall rise.
2. And shall have the mar-riage sup-per [*Omit* . . .] dead shall rise, in the skies, up in the skies.

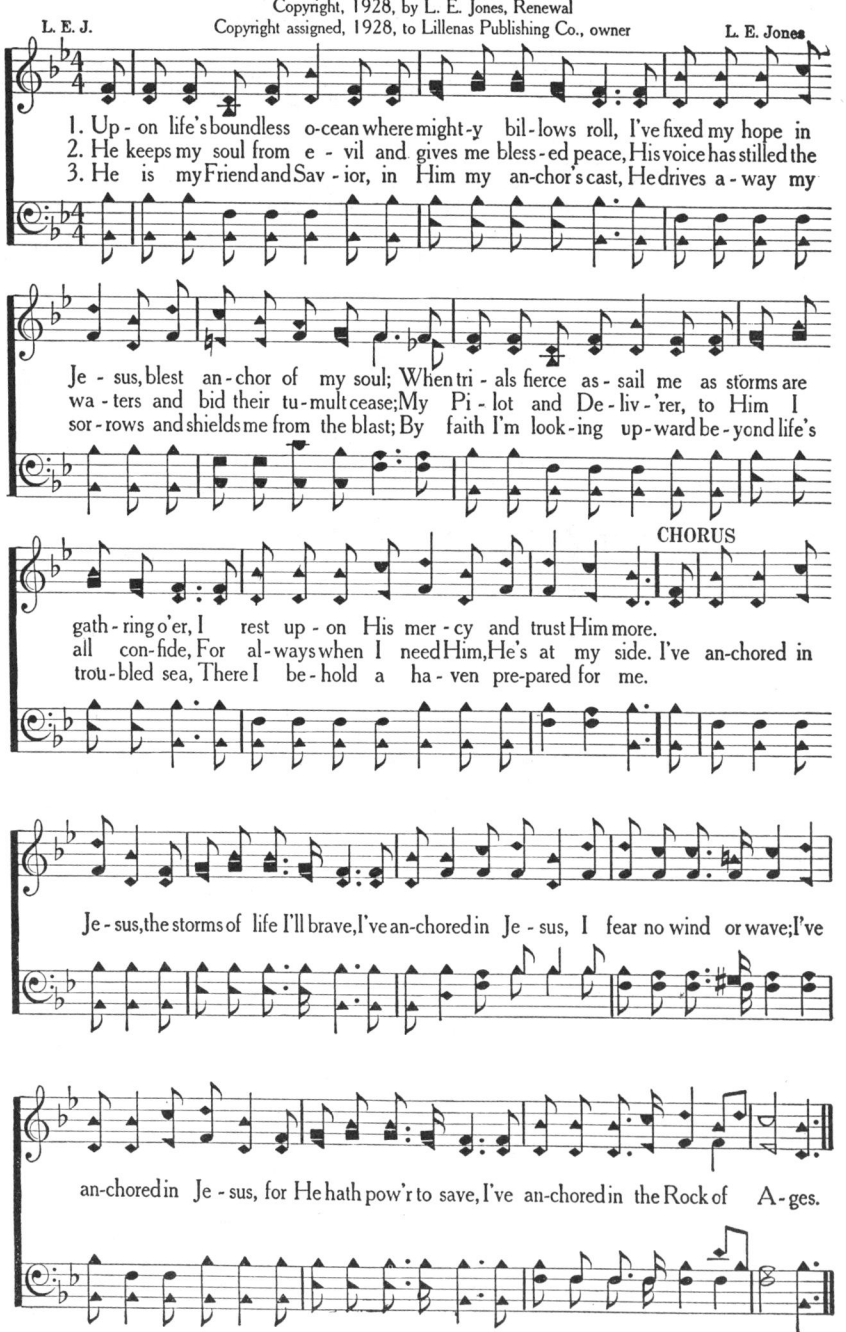

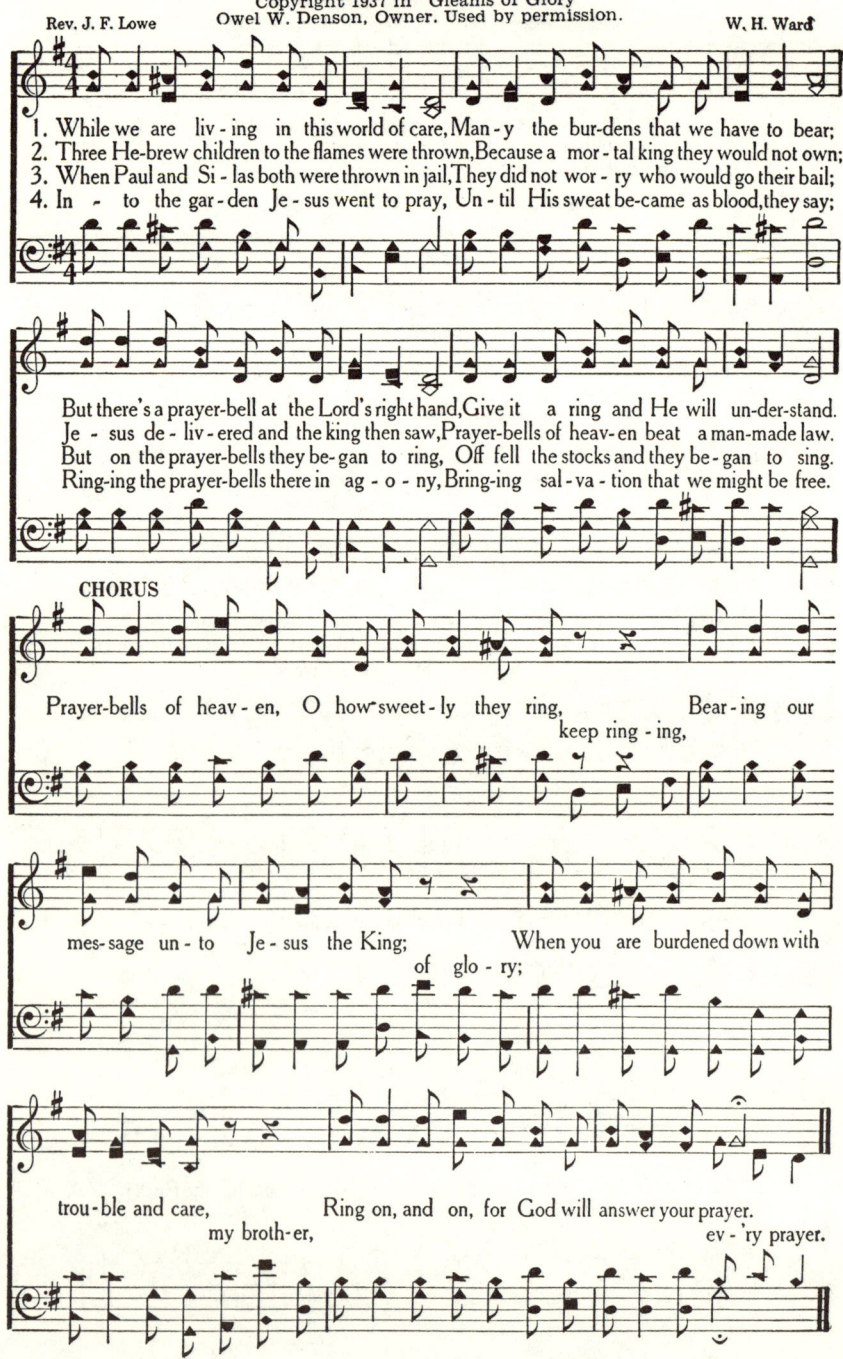

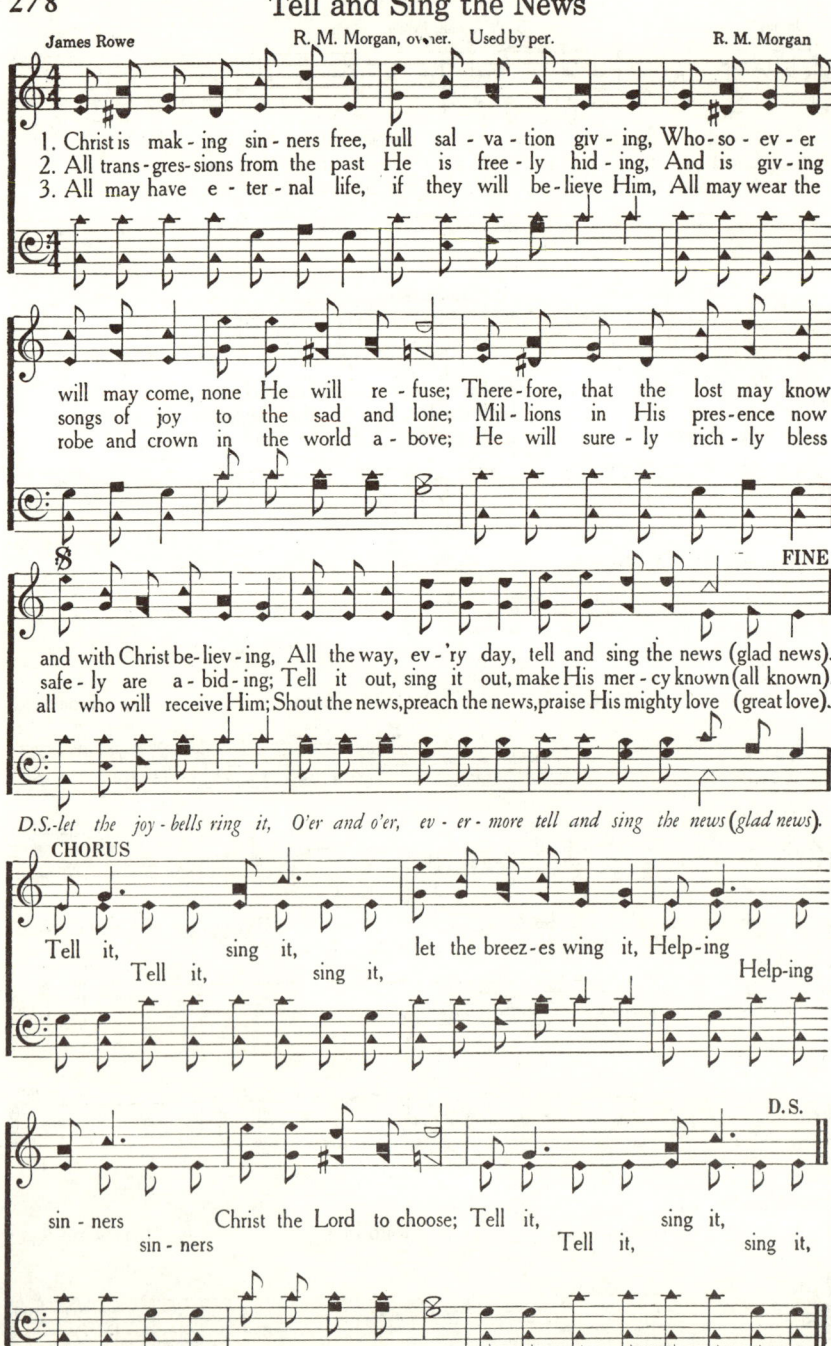

Lord, I Believe

283

Harmony by R. E. W.
Arr. by F. M. G. and A. F. I.

1. When sorrow and storms are besetting my track, And Satan is whisp'ring "You'd better turn back", How oft I have proved it, tho' dark be the way, A little believing drives clouds all away.
2. How easy when sailing the sea in a calm, To trust in the strength of Jehovah's great arm; But somehow I find when the waves swamp the boat, It takes some believing to keep things afloat.
3. "I'll stand to the end", I have heard people say, "I'll fight till I die, and will ne'er run away"; But when by temptation so fiercely assailed, They left off believing, and terribly failed.
4. And others there are full of courage and zeal, Who go to the battle like warriors of steel; But right in the heat of the conflict with sin, Instead of believing, they faint and give in.
5. Then let us remember in running this race, That faith is not feeling, and trust is not trace; And when all around us seems dark as the night, We'll keep on believing, and win in the fight.

REFRAIN

Lord, I believe, Lord, I believe! Savior, raise my faith in Thee, Till it can move a mountain; Lord, I believe, Lord, I believe! All my doubts are buried in the fountain.

Wonderful Power In the Blood! 289

"Without shedding of blood is no remission."—Heb. 9: 22

R. E. W.
R. E. Winsett, owner
R. E. Winsett. By per.

1. There is won-der-work-ing pow'r in the precious blood, There is pow'r in the blood; It will cleanse from ev-'ry sin, It will make you pure with-in,
2. Praise the Fa-ther and the Son for the sac-ri-fice, That was made for you and me, That from sin we might be free,
3. When we at the judgment stand, blood will be our plea, There's no oth-er way I know, But this pre-cious crim-son flow,
4. O our Savior's precious blood flow'd for all the world, 'Tis sal-va-tion's won-drous plan, That was made for ev-'ry man,
5. Who-so-ev-er will may come to this precious blood, There is pow'r in the blood; Sin-ner, do not long-er wait, For the judg-ment seals thy fate,

CHORUS

There is pow'r in the blood. Won-der-ful pow'r in the blood,
There is pow'r in the blood of the Lamb. Won-der-ful pow'r in the blood of the Lamb,

There is per-fect cleans-ing pow'r in the
O the blood has won-der-ful pow'r,

pre-cious blood; There is won-der-work-ing pow'r in the blood (of the Lamb).

290. Wonderful Peace

W. D. Cornell, Alt.
W. G. Cooper

1. Far a-way in the depth of my spir-it to-night Rolls a mel-o-dy sweet-er than psalm; In ce-les-tial like strains it un-ceas-ing-ly falls O'er my soul like an in-fi-nite calm.
2. What a treas-ure I have in this won-der-ful peace, Bur-ied deep in the heart of my soul; So se-cure that no pow-er can mine it a-way, While the years of e-ter-ni-ty roll.
3. I am rest-ing to-night in this won-der-ful peace, Rest-ing sweet-ly in Je-sus' con-trol; For I'm kept from all dan-ger by night and by day, And His glo-ry is flood-ing my soul.
4. And me-thinks when I rise to that cit-y of peace, Where the Au-thor of peace I shall see, That one strain of the song which the ran-somed will sing, In that heav-en-ly king-dom shall be.
5. Ah! soul, are you here with-out com-fort and rest, March-ing down the rough path-way of time? Make Je-sus your Friend ere the shad-ows grow dark, O, ac-cept this sweet peace so sub-lime.

CHORUS

Peace! peace! won-der-ful peace, Com-ing down from the Fa-ther a-bove; Sweep o-ver my spir-it for-ev-er, I pray, In fath-om-less bil-lows of love.

294 When They Ring the Golden Bells

Copyright, 1887, by Dion DeMarbelle. Used by permission of the John Church Co., owners of copyright

Dion DeMarbelle

1. There's a land be-yond the riv-er, That we call the sweet for-ev-er, And we
2. We shall know no sin nor sor-row, In that ha-ven of to-mor-row, When our
3. When our days shall know their num-ber, When in death we sweet-ly slum-ber, When the

on-ly reach that shore by faith's de-cree; One by one we'll gain the por-tals, There to
barque shall sail be-yond the sil-ver sea; We shall on-ly know the bless-ing Of our
King commands the spir-it to be free; Nev-er-more with an-guish la-den, We shall

FINE

dwell with the im-mor-tals, When they ring the gold-en bells for you and me.
Fa-ther's sweet ca-ress-ing, When they ring the gold-en bells for you and me.
reach that love-ly ai-den, When they ring the gold-en bells for you and me. you and me.

D.S.-yond the shin-ing riv-er When they ring the gold-en bells for you and me.

CHORUS

Don't you hear the bells now ring-ing? Don't you hear the an-gels sing-ing? 'Tis the

D.S.

glo-ry hal-le-lu-jah Ju-bi-lee (Ju-bi-lee), In the far-off sweet for-ev-er, Just be-

When I Make My Last Move

295

International Copyright, MCMXXXIX. Owned and controlled by R. E. Winsett, Dayton, Tenn.
Words and Mel. by Herbert Buffum
Copyright, 1926, by Mrs. John A. Anderson
Har. by R. E. Winsett

1. I've been trav-'ling for Je-sus so much of my life, I've been trav-'ling on land and on sea; But I'm count-ing on tak-ing a trip to the sky, That will be the last move for me.
2. I've seen won-der-ful sights as I've trav-eled a-far, But how lit-tle, how emp-ty 'twill seem; When I make my last move to that cit-y of gold, And be-hold what no vi-sion could dream.
3. There'll be prophets of yore, whom I'll meet o-ver there, And whose teachings have guid-ed me right; I shall meet the a-pos-tles and Je-sus my Lord, I be-lieve I shall know them at sight.
4. Here I'm both-ered with pack-ing each time that I move, And I car-ry a load in each hand; But I'll not need one thing I have used in this world, When I move to that heav-en-ly land.

CHORUS

When I move to the sky, up to heav-en on high, What a won-der-ful trip that will be! I'm all read-y to go, washed in Cal-va-ry's flow; That will be the last move for me.

296 When Jesus Comes In the Clouds

Copyright, 1941, by Tennessee Music and Printing Co., in "New Found Joy"

A. F.   Allan Frazier

1. O what a shout will rise a-cross the vault-ed skies, When Jesus comes in the clouds; We'll leave all pain and care, and end-less glo-ry share, When Je-sus comes in the clouds.......
2. All war and strife will cease, there'll be e-ter-nal peace, Up-on the hills of home our feet shall ev-er roam,
3. With all the friends of old, we'll tread the streets of gold, When Je-sus comes in the clouds; There'll be no more good-byes, no tears will dim our eyes, When Je-sus comes

D. S.—All sor-row will be past, e-ter-nal joy at last,

FINE

CHORUS

When Je-sus comes.......... in glo-ry bright;........ We'll leave the lone - - - - - ly shades of night;........... D. S.

298   What a Happy Time

J. M. Henson   Copyright, 1933, in "Songs of Praise No. 2." Owned by Morris-Henson & Cook   J. T. Cook

1. Sor-rows of-ten meet us here, Bur-dens press us so, And the way is hard to see That we have to go, But we press a-long in faith To our home a-bove, Let-ting Je-sus lead us on, Rest-ing in His love.
2. We will la-bor, watch and pray, As we go a-long, Let-ting Je-sus lead the way, Keep-ing cour-age strong, Know-ing that we shall reach home By His grace sub-lime, When we are all gath-ered there, What a hap-py time.
3. Come and join us on our march To that hap-py place, Where we shall ex-tol our Lord, Look-ing on His face, Shar-ing all the joys up there In that sun-ny clime, Prais-ing Je-sus ev-er-more, What a hap-py time.

D.S.- Sing-ing while the a-ges roll, What a hap-py time.

CHORUS

What a hap-py time 'twill be When we all get home, O-ver by the crys-tal sea, Nev-er-more to roam; In that home-land of the soul, Where the joy-bells chime,

302 We Are Going Down the Valley

Jessie H. Brown   Copyright, 1918, by Fillmore Brothers Co., Renewal. Lillenas Pub. Co., owner   J. H. Fillmore

1. We are go-ing down the val-ley one by one, With our fac-es t'ward the set-ting of the sun; Down the val-ley where the mourn-ful cy-press grows, Where the stream of death in si-lence on-ward flows.

2. We are go-ing down the val-ley one by one, When the la-bors of the wea-ry day are done; One by one the cares of earth for-ev-er past, We shall stand up-on the riv-er bank at last.

3. We are go-ing down the val-ley one by one, Hu-man com-rade you or I will there have none; But a ten-der hand will guide us lest we fall, Christ is go-ing down the val-ley with us all.

CHORUS

We are go-ing down the val-ley, go-ing down the val-ley, Go-ing t'ward the set-ting of the sun; We are go-ing down the val-ley, go-ing down the val-ley, Go-ing down the val-ley one by one.

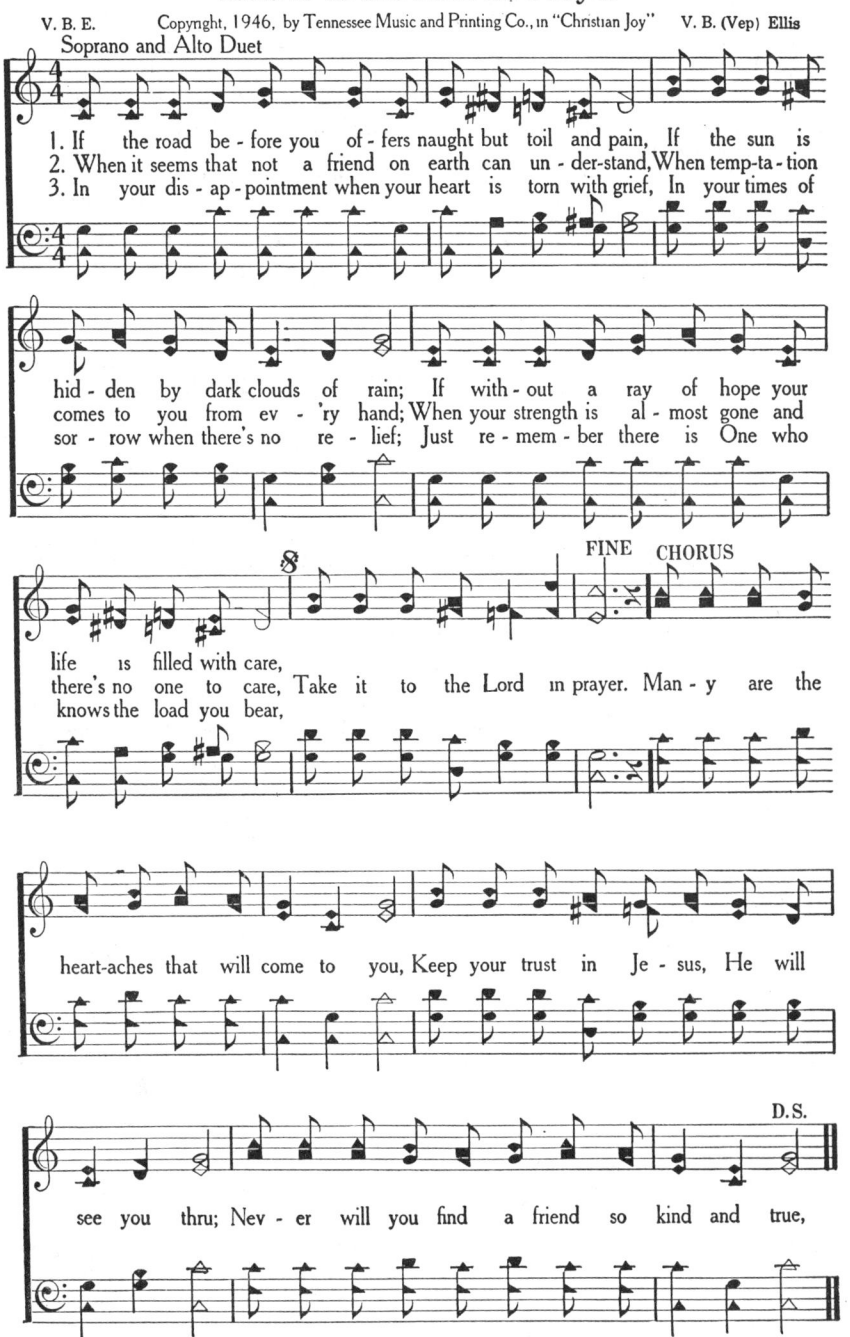

His Love Lights the Way

317

A. F.   Copyright, 1938, in "Living Presents," by Tennessee Music and Printing Co.   Allen Frazier

1. I've left the old paths I trav-eled so long, I'm hap-py, redeemed and free;
Of Je-sus the Lord I sing a sweet song, His love lights the way for me.

2. The pleas-ures of sin no more I de-sire, No good in them now I see;
The Spir-it has set my be-ing on fire,

3. Each tri-al o'er-come adds strength to my soul, And faith-ful I'll ev-er be;
The bil-lows of grace now o-ver me roll, for me.

CHORUS

His love lights the way,   I trav-el to-day,
His love lights the way,   I trav-el to-day,

I'm shouting the vic-to-ry;   My sad-ness is past, I'm
the vic-to-ry; My sad-ness is past,

I'm hap-py at last, His love lights the way for me.
hap-py at last,   for me.

318 My Sins Are Gone

N.B.V.   Copyright, 1934, by Harry D. Clarke, Winona Lake, Ind. Used by per.   N. B. Vandall

1. You ask why I am hap-py so I'll just tell you why, Be-cause my sins are gone; And when I meet the scof-fers who ask me where they are, I say, my sins are gone.
2. 'Twas at the old-time al-tar where God came in my heart, And now my sins are gone; The Lord took full pos-ses-sion, the dev-il did de-part, I'm glad my sins are gone.
3. When Sa-tan comes to tempt me and tries to make me doubt, I say, my sins are gone; You got me in-to trou-ble, but Je-sus got me out, I'm glad my sins are gone.
4. I'm liv-ing now for Je-sus, I'm hap-py night and day, Be-cause my sins are gone; My soul is filled with mu-sic, with all my heart I say, I know my sins are gone.

CHORUS

They're un-der-neath the Blood, on the Cross of Cal-va-ry, As far re-moved as dark-ness is from dawn; In the sea of God's for-get-ful-ness, that's good e-nough for me, Praise God, my sins are gone.

322 Working For the Crown

Mrs. H. A. Mabry   Copyright, 1899, by H. A. R. Horton   H. A. R. Horton

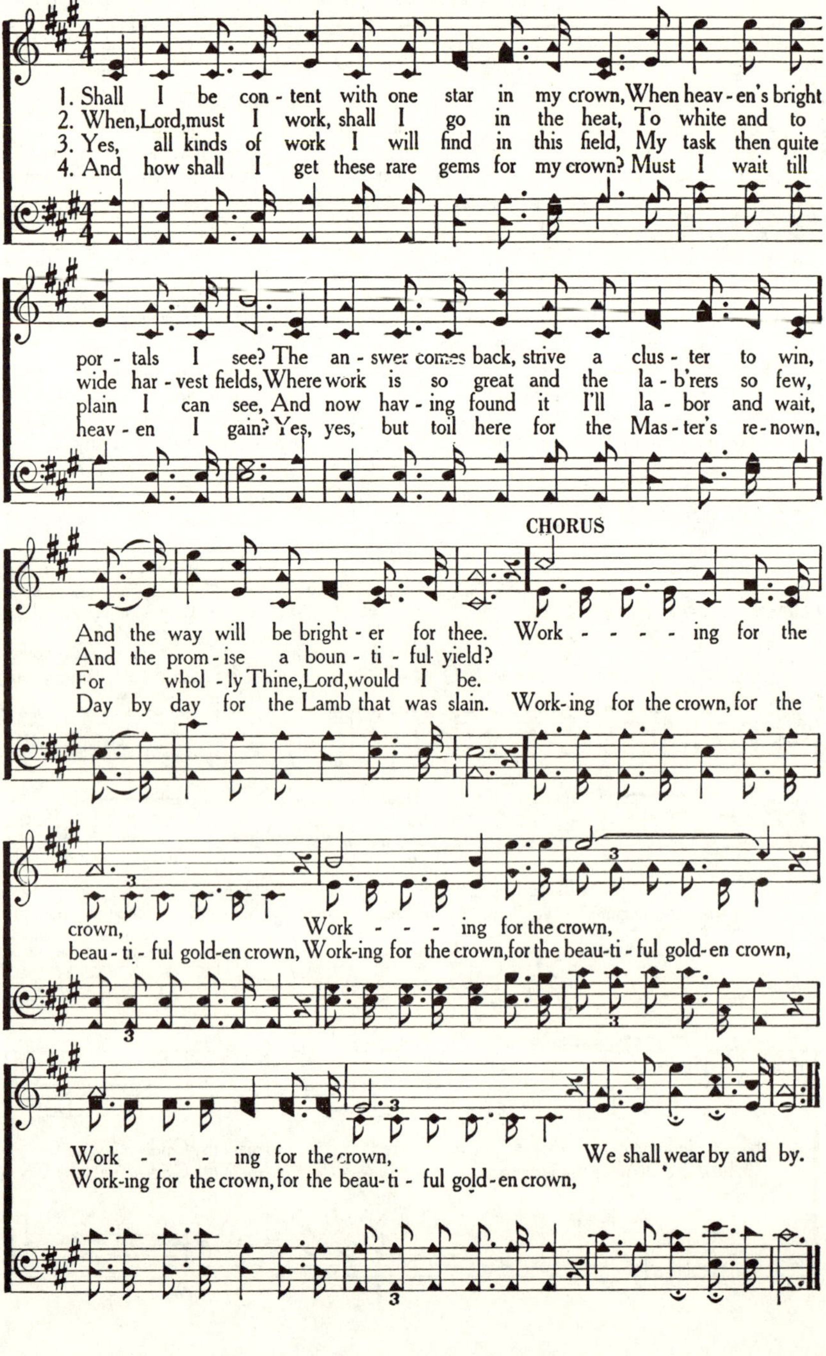

1. Shall I be content with one star in my crown, When heaven's bright portals I see? The answer comes back, strive a cluster to win, And the way will be brighter for thee.
2. When, Lord, must I work, shall I go in the heat, To white and to wide harvest fields, Where work is so great and the lab'rers so few, And the promise a bountiful yield?
3. Yes, all kinds of work I will find in this field, My task then quite plain I can see, And now having found it I'll labor and wait, For wholly Thine, Lord, would I be.
4. And how shall I get these rare gems for my crown? Must I wait till heaven I gain? Yes, yes, but toil here for the Master's renown, Day by day for the Lamb that was slain.

CHORUS

Working for the crown, for the beautiful golden crown, Working for the crown, for the beautiful golden crown, Working for the crown, We shall wear by and by.

332 Swing the Door Open Wide

"If a man hear my voice and open the door, I will come in."—Rev. 1:20

Lizzie DeArmond
Chas. W. Vaughan

1. Swing the door of your heart o-pen wide, Let the Sav-ior of sin-ners with-in;
2. Swing the door of your heart o-pen wide, Hear His voice ring-ing out clear and sweet;
3. Swing the door of your heart o-pen wide, Do not grieve Him by turn-ing a-way;

Bid Him en-ter and with you a-bide, Give you grace a new life to be-gin.
There's a won-der-ful Friend just out-side, Haste with glad-ness your dear Lord to greet.
Long with pa-tience He's wait-ed out-side, He will give you a bless-ing to-day.

D. S.- Sav-ior come in to a-bide.

CHORUS

Swing it wide, swing it wide, Swing the door of your heart o-pen
Swing it wide, swing it wide,

wide; Swing it wide, swing it wide, Bid the
swing it wide; Swing it wide, swing it wide,

THE B-I-B-L-E

Have boys and girls raise Bibles high in air during singing of this chorus.

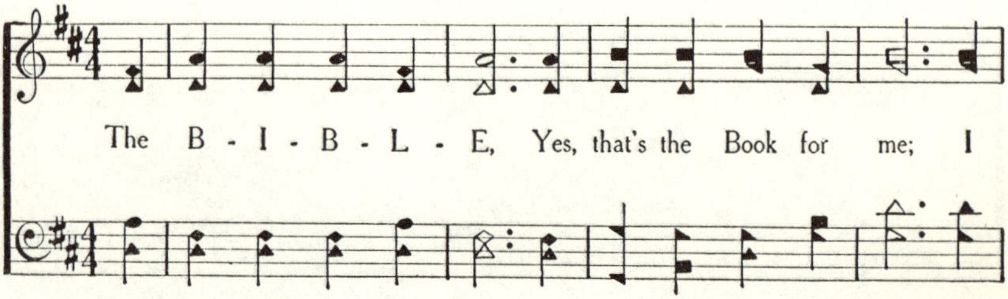

The B - I - B - L - E, Yes, that's the Book for me; I

336 Jesus Forgives And Forgets

Rev. Johnson Oatman, Jr.   G. Kieffer Vaughan, owner. 1923.   G. Kieffer Vaughan

1. Praise the Lord there is mer-cy in heav-en, In that land where the sun nev-er sets;
2. When we bowed at the foot-stool of mer-cy, When we knocked on the door to get in;
3. Oft we hear peo-ple say, "I'll for-give you, But I can-not for-get if I tried;"
4. When our Book shall be o-pened for judgment, May we find there no rec-ord of debts;

For the Sav-ior for-gives, not as mor-tals, But our Je-sus for-gives and for-gets.
Je-sus not on-ly free-ly did par-don, But for-gave and for-got ev-'ry sin.
But our Savior's own blood sealed our ransom, To for-give and for-get He hath died.
We'll not fear if our sins have been pardoned, For our Je-sus for-gives and for-gets.

CHORUS

He for-gives and for-gets, He for-gives and for-gets,
He forgives and He for-gets, yes, He forgives and He for-gets,
Not as mor-tals for-give one an-oth-er, But our Je-sus forgives and for-gets.

Take Me As I Am

J. H. S.   J. H. Stockton

1. Je-sus my Lord, to Thee I cry; Un-less Thou help me I must die;
2. Help-less I am and full of guilt, But yet Thy blood was for me spilt;
3. No prep-a-ra-tion can I make, My best re-solves I on-ly break;
4. I thirst, I long to know Thy love, Thy full sal-va-tion I would prove;

338. Honey In the Rock

F. A. G. — F. A. Graves

1. O my broth-er, do you know the Sav-ior, Who is won-drous, kind and true?
2. Have you "Tasted that the Lord is gracious?" Do you walk in the way that's new?
3. Do you pray un-to God the Father, "What wilt Thou have me to do?"
4. Then go out thru the streets and byways, Preach the Word to the man-y or few;

He's the "Rock of your sal-va-tion!"
Have you drunk from the liv-ing foun-tain? There's Honey in the Rock for you.
Nev-er fear, He will sure-ly an-swer,
Say to ev-'ry fall-en broth-er,

CHORUS

O, there's Honey in the Rock, my broth-er, There's Hon-ey in the Rock for my brother, you; Leave your sins for the blood to cov-er, There's Hon-ey in the Rock for you. for you;

Let It Shine On Me

M. S. L. — Tennessee Music and Printing Co., owner — M. S. Lemons

1. Out on life's o-cean far from the shore, Let the light from the light-house
2. Waft-ed by bil-lows, tossed by the sea, Let the light from the light-house

This Little Light of Mine

343

This lit-tle light of mine, Yes! I'm gon-na let it shine;
Hide it un-der a bush-el? No! I'm gon-na let it shine;
Won't let Sa - - tan blow it out, I'm gon-na let it shine;
Shine all o - ver(★)Chi - ca - go, Yes! I'm gon-na let it shine;
Let it shine till Je - sus comes, I'm gon-na let it shine;

Let it shine, let it shine, let it shine.

★ Substitute local name

O Happy Day

Philip Doddridge E. F. Rimbault

1. { O hap-py day that fixed my choice On Thee, my Sav - ior and my God!
   { Well may this glow - ing heart re - joice, And tell its rap - tures all a - broad.
2. { O hap-py bond that seals my vows To Him Who mer - its all my love!
   { Let cheer-ful an - thems fill His house, While to that sa - cred shrine I move.
3. { 'Tis done: the great trans-ac - tion's done; I am my Lord's, and He is mine;
   { He drew me and I fol-lowed on, Charmed to con - fess the voice di - vine.
4. { Now rest, my long - di - vid - ed heart; Fixed on this bliss - ful cen - ter rest;
   { Nor ev - er from my Lord de - part, With Him of ev - 'ry good pos-sessed.

FINE

Hap - py day, hap - py day, When Je - sus washed my sins a - way!

D.S.

He taught me how to watch and pray, And live re - joic - ing ev - 'ry day;

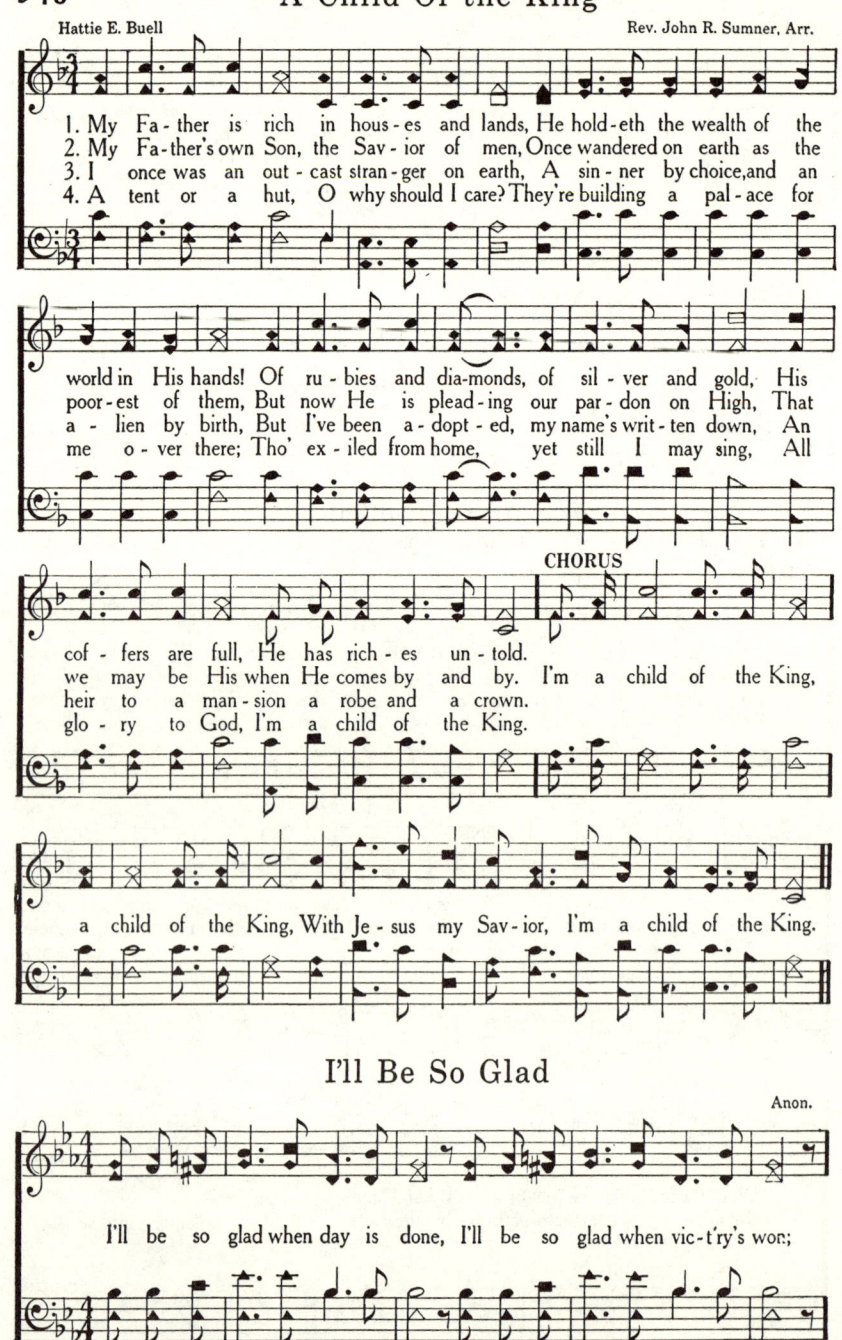

Sweet By-and-By

351

For the Fa-ther waits o-ver the way, To pre-pare us a dwell-ing place there.
And our spir-its shall sor-row no more, Not a sigh for the bless-ing of rest.
For the glo-ri-ous gift of His love, And the bless-ings that hal-low our days.

CHORUS

In the sweet by-and-by, We shall meet on that beau-ti-ful shore; by-and-by;

In the sweet by and by, We shall meet on that beau-ti-ful shore.

The Old-Time Religion

Old Melody

1. Makes me love ev-'ry-bod-y, Makes me love ev-'ry-
2. It was good for our moth-ers, It was good for our
3. It was good for our fa-thers, It was good for our
4. It will do when I am dy-ing, It will do when I am
5. It will take us all to heav-en, It will take us all to

Cho.—'Tis the old-time re-li-gion, 'Tis the old-time re-

D. C. for Cho.

bod-y, Makes me love ev-'ry-bod-y, It's good e-nough for me.
moth-ers, It was good for our moth-ers, It's good e-nough for me.
fa-thers, It was good for our fa-thers, It's good e-nough for me.
dy-ing, It will do when I am dy-ing, It's good e-nough for me.
heav-en, It will take us all to heav-en, It's good e-nough for me.

li-gion, 'Tis the old time re-li-gion, It's good e-nough for me.

Hold to God's Unchanging Hand

359

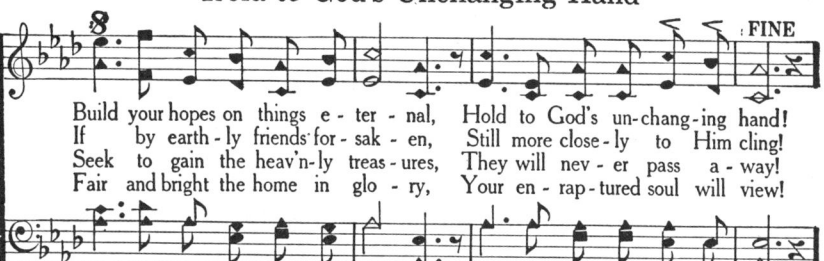

1. Build your hopes on things e-ter-nal, Hold to God's un-chang-ing hand!
2. If by earth-ly friends for-sak-en, Still more close-ly to Him cling!
3. Seek to gain the heav'n-ly treas-ures, They will nev-er pass a-way!
4. Fair and bright the home in glo-ry, Your en-rap-tured soul will view!

D.S.- Build your hopes on things e-ter-nal, Hold to God's un-chang-ing hand!

CHORUS

Hold to God's un-changing hand! Hold to God's un-changing hand!
Hold to His hand, Hold to His hand,

Leaning On the Everlasting Arms

Rev. E. A. Hoffman   Tennessee Music and Printing Co., owner   A. J. Showalter

1. What a fel-low-ship, what a joy di-vine, Lean-ing on the ev-er-
   What a bless-ed-ness, what a peace is mine, Lean-ing on the ev-er-
2. O how sweet to walk in this pil-grim way, Lean-ing on the ev-er-
   O how bright the path grows from day to day, Lean-ing on the ev-er-
3. What have I to dread, what have I to fear, Lean-ing on the ev-er-
   I have bless-ed peace with my Lord so near, Lean-ing on the ev-er-

CHORUS

last-ing arms; Lean - - - ing, lean - - - ing,
last - - - ing arms. Lean-ing on Je-sus, lean-ing on Je-sus,

Safe and se-cure from all a-larms; Lean-ing on the ev-er-last-ing arms.

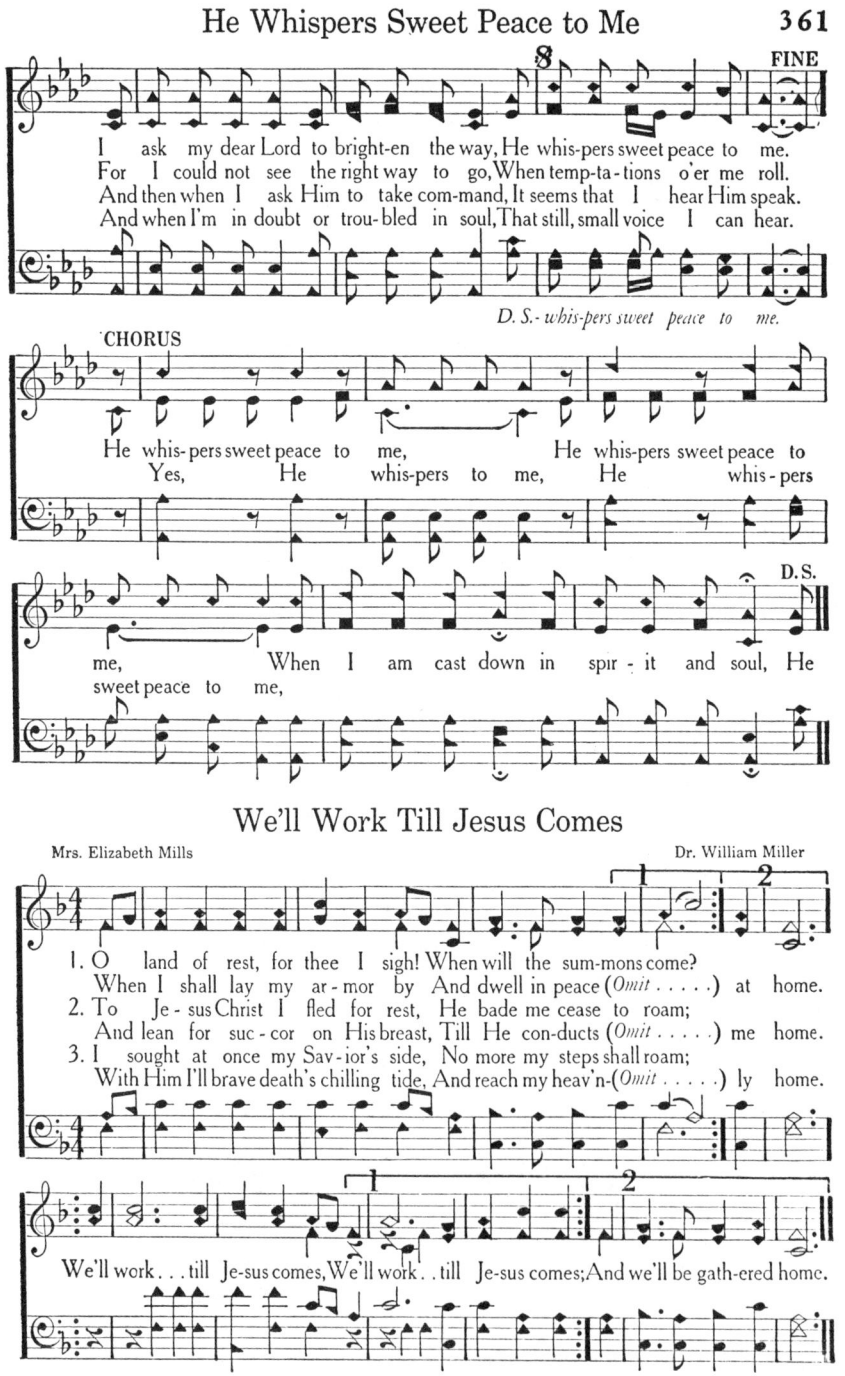

362 I Am Thine, O Lord

F. J. Crosby
Copyright, 1875, by Biglow and Main
W. H. Doane

1. I am Thine, O Lord, I have heard Thy voice, And it told Thy love to me;
2. Con-se-crate me now to Thy serv-ice, Lord, By the pow'r of grace di-vine;
3. O the pure de-light of a sin-gle hour, That be-fore Thy throne I spend;
4. There are depths of love that I can-not know, Till I cross the nar-row sea;

But I long to rise in the arms of faith, And be clos-er drawn to Thee.
Let my soul look up with a stead-fast hope, And my will be lost in Thine.
When I kneel in prayer, and with Thee, my God, I com-mune as friend with friend.
There are heights of joy that I may not reach, Till I rest in peace with Thee.

CHORUS

Draw me near-er, near-er, bless-ed Lord, To the cross where Thou hast died;
Near-er, near-er,
Draw me near-er, near-er, near-er, bless-ed Lord, To Thy pre-cious, bleeding side.

God Calling Yet

"I have called, and ye have refused."—Prov. 1:24
This hymn is free to be used for the glory of God.

J. Borthwick
John

1. God call-ing yet! shall I not hear? Earth's pleasures shall I still hold dear?
2. God call-ing yet! shall I not rise? Can I His lov-ing voice de-spise,
3. God call-ing yet! and shall I give No heed, but still in bond-age live?
4. God call-ing yet! I can-not stay; My heart I yield with-out de-lay;

370 O, Why Not Tonight?

Re-entered and Copyright, 1895, by J. H. Hall
J. Calvin Bushey

1. O, do not let the word de-part, And close thine eyes a-gainst the light; Poor sin-ner, hard-en not your heart, Be saved, O, to-night.
2. To-mor-row's sun may nev-er rise, To bless thy long-de-lud-ed sight; This is the time, O then be wise, Be saved, O, to-night.
3. Our Lord in pit-y lin-gers still, And wilt thou thus His love re-quite? Re-nounce at once thy stub-born will, Be saved, O, to-night.
4. Our bless-ed Lord re-fus-ed none Who would to Him their souls u-nite; Be-lieve, o-bey, the work is done, Be saved, O, to-night.

CHORUS

O, why not to-night? O, why not to-night?
O, why not to-night? why not to-night? why not to-night?
night? Wilt thou be saved? Then why not to-night?
why not tonight? Wilt thou be sav'd, wilt thou be sav'd? Then why not, O why not to-night?

Revive Us Again

Wm. P. Mackay
J. J. Husband

1. We praise Thee, O God, for the Son of Thy love, For Je-sus who died and is now gone a-bove.
2. All glory and praise to the Lamb that was slain, Who has borne all our sins and has cleans'd ev'ry stain.
3. Re-vive us again, fill each heart with Thy love, May each soul be re-kin-dled with fire from a-bove.

Revive Us Again

371

CHORUS

Hal-le-lu-jah! Thine the glo-ry, Hal-le-lu-jah! a-men; Re-vive us a-gain.

O Little Town of Bethlehem

Phillips Brooks   Lewis H. Redner

1. O lit-tle town of Beth-le-hem! How still we see thee lie; A-bove thy deep and dream-less sleep, The si-lent stars go by; Yet in thy dark streets shin-eth, The ev-er-last-ing light; The hopes and fears of all the years, Are met in thee to-night.
2. For Christ is born of Ma-ry, And gath-ered all a-bove; While mor-tals sleep, the an-gels keep, Their watch of won-d'ring love; O morn-ing stars, to-geth-er, Pro-claim the ho-ly birth! And prais-es sing to God the King, And peace to men on earth.
3. How si-lent-ly, how si-lent-ly The won-drous gift is giv'n! So God im-parts to hu-man heart, The bless-ing of His heav'n; No ear may hear His com-ing, But in this world of sin, Where meek souls will re-ceive Him still, The dear Christ en-ters in.
4. O ho-ly Child of Beth-le-hem! De-scend to us, we pray; Cast out our sin and en-ter in, Be born in us to-day; We hear the Christ-mas an-gels, The great glad ti-dings tell; O come to us, a-bide with us, Our Lord Im-man-u-el!

372 Onward, Christian Soldiers

Sabine Gould — First Tune — *Sir Arthur Sullivan*

1. On-ward, Christian sol-diers! Marching as to war, With the cross of Je-sus
2. At the sign of tri-umph, Sa-tan's host doth flee; On, then, Christian sol-diers,
3. Like a might-y ar-my Moves the church of God; Broth-ers we are tread-ing
4. On-ward, then, ye peo-ple, Join our hap-py throng, Blend with ours your voic-es

Go-ing on be-fore; Christ the roy-al Mas-ter, Leads a-gainst the foe;
On to vic-to-ry! Hell's foun-da-tions quiv-er At the shout of praise;
Where the saints have trod; We are not di-vid-ed, All one bod-y we,
In the tri-umph song; Glo-ry, laud and hon-or Un-to Christ the King,

CHORUS

For-ward in-to bat-tle, See His ban-ner go!
Broth-ers, lift your voic-es, Loud your an-thems raise. On-ward, Chris-tian
One in hope and doc-trine, One in char-i-ty.
This thru count-less a-ges Men and an-gels sing.

sol-diers! Marching as to war, With the cross of Je-sus go-ing on be-fore.

O Say, But I'm Glad

Arr. by C. T. — Copyright, 1936, in "Homeland Harmony" — *Arr. by Curtis Taylor*

1. There is a won-der-ful song in my heart, Something I once did not have;
2. Won-der-ful love He so free-ly did bring, In-to my heart that was sad;
3. O the sweet fel-low-ship I now en-joy, For I no long-er feel sad;

There's a Great Day Coming

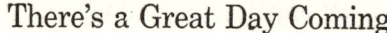

W. L. T. By per. W. F. Thompson & Co., East Liverpool, O., and Chicago W. L. Thompson

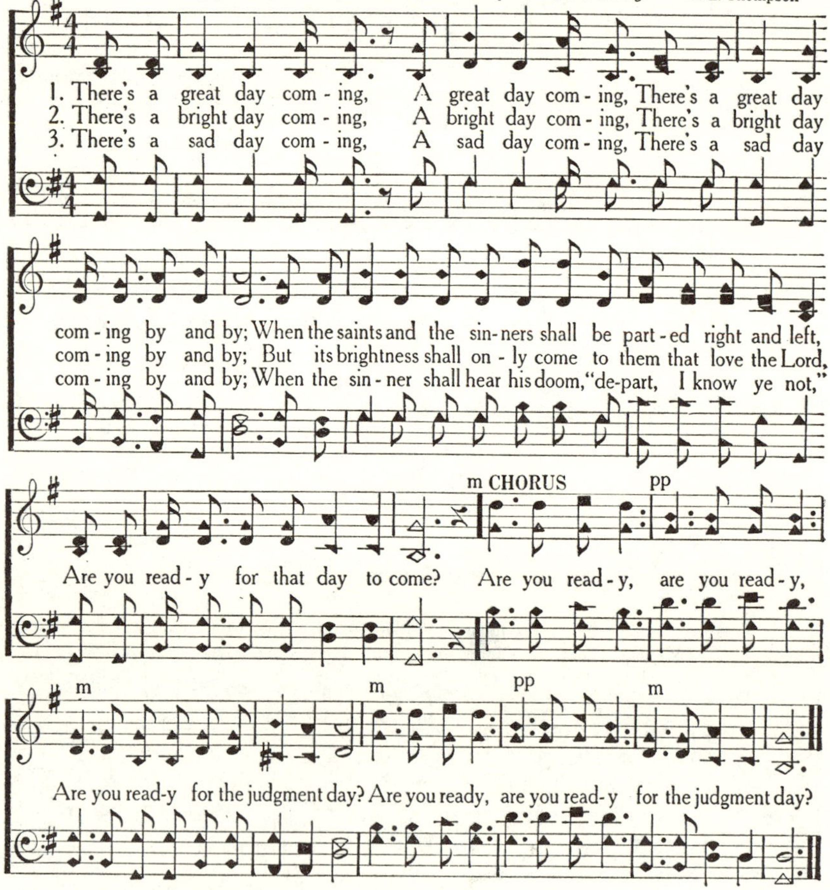

1. There's a great day com - ing, A great day com - ing, There's a great day
2. There's a bright day com - ing, A bright day com - ing, There's a bright day
3. There's a sad day com - ing, A sad day com - ing, There's a sad day
com - ing by and by; When the saints and the sin - ners shall be part - ed right and left,
com - ing by and by; But its brightness shall on - ly come to them that love the Lord,
com - ing by and by; When the sin - ner shall hear his doom, "de-part, I know ye not,"
Are you read - y for that day to come?
m CHORUS
Are you read - y, pp are you read - y,
m Are you read-y for the judgment day? m Are you ready, pp are you read- y m for the judgment day?

Yield Not To Temptation

H. R. P. "Watch ye and pray, lest ye enter into temptation."- Mark 14: 38. H. R. Palmer

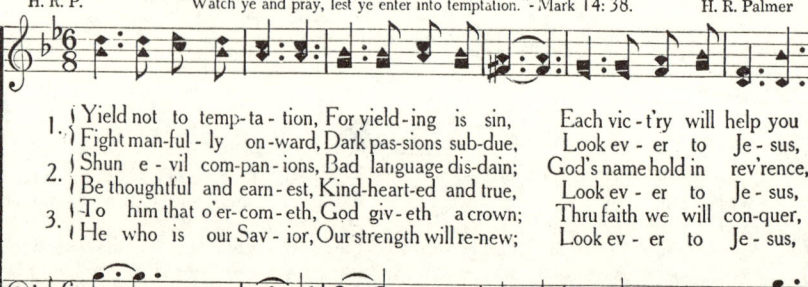

1. Yield not to temp-ta - tion, For yield - ing is sin, Each vic - t'ry will help you
Fight man-ful - ly on-ward, Dark pas-sions sub-due, Look ev - er to Je - sus,
2. Shun e - vil com-pan - ions, Bad language dis-dain; God's name hold in rev'rence,
Be thoughtful and earn - est, Kind-heart-ed and true, Look ev - er to Je - sus,
3. To him that o'er-com - eth, God giv - eth a crown; Thru faith we will con-quer,
He who is our Sav - ior, Our strength will re-new; Look ev - er to Je - sus,

382 The Last Mile of the Way

Johnson Oatman, Jr. Copyright, 1936, W. E. Marks, renewal. John T. Benson, Jr., owner Wm. Edie Marks

1. If I walk in the pathway of du-ty, If I work till the close of the day,
2. If for Christ I proclaim the glad sto-ry, If I seek for His sheep gone a-stray,
3. Here the dear-est of ties we must sev-er, Tears of sor-row are seen ev-'ry day,
4. And if here I have earn-est-ly striv-en, And have tried all His will to o-bey,

FINE

I shall see the great King in His beau-ty,
I am sure He will show me His glo-ry, When I've gone the last mile of the way.
But no sick-ness, no sigh-ing for-ev-er,
'Twill enhance all the rap-ture of heav-en,

CHORUS

When I've gone the last mile of the way, I will rest at the
    the last mile of the way,

D.S.

close of the day, And I know there are joys that a-wait me,
  at the close of the day,

I Would Not Be Denied

C. P. J. (Gen. 32: 24-28) C. P. Jones

1. When pangs of death seized on my soul, Un-to the Lord I cried,
2. As Ja-cob in the days of old, I wres-tled with the Lord,
3. Old Sa-tan said my Lord was gone And would not hear my prayer,

388. Throw Out the Life-Line

Rev. E. S. U.
Rev. E. S. Ufford

1. Throw out the life-line a-cross the dark wave, There is a broth-er whom some-one should save; Some-bod-y's broth-er, O who then will dare To throw out the life-line, his per-il to share?
2. Throw out the life-line with hand quick and strong, Why do you tar-ry, my broth-er, so long? See, he is sink-ing, O has-ten to-day, And out with the life-boat, a-way, a-way.
3. Throw out the life-line to dan-ger-fraught men, Sink-ing in an-guish where we've nev-er been; Winds of temp-ta-tion and bil-lows of woe, Will soon hurl them out where the dark wa-ters flow.
4. Soon will this sea-son of res-cue be o'er, Soon we shall go to the fair E-den shore; Then in the dark hour of death may it be, That Je-sus will throw out the life-line to thee.

CHORUS

Throw out the life-line! throw out the life-line! Some-one is drift-ing a-way, Some-one is sink-ing to-day.

O Come All Ye Faithful

1. O come, all ye faith-ful, Joy-ful and tri-um-phant, O come ye, O come ye to
2. Sing, choirs of an-gels, Sing in ex-ul-ta-tion, O sing, all ye bright hosts of
3. Yea, Lord, we greet Thee, born this happy morn-ing, O Je-sus, to Thee be all

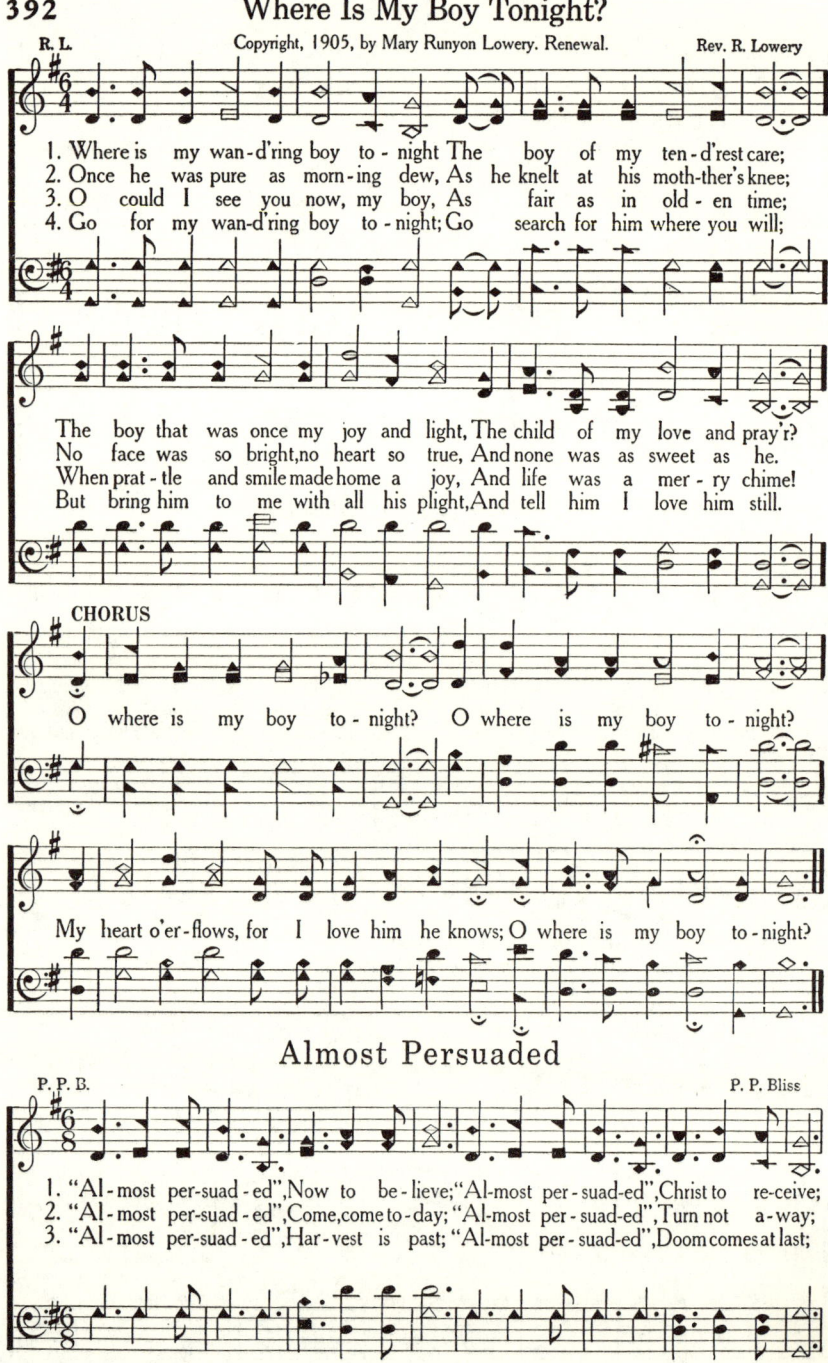

Almost Persuaded

Seems now some soul to say, "Go, Spir-it, go Thy way, Some more convenient day On Thee I'll call".
Je - sus invites you here, Angels are ling'ring near, Pray'rs rise from hearts so dear; O wand'rer come!
"Al - most" can-not a-vail; "Al-most" is but to fail, Sad, sad that bit-ter wail, "Al-most, but lost".

When We all Get to Heaven

E. E. Hewitt Copyright, 1898, by Mrs. J. G. Wilson Mrs. J. G. Wilson

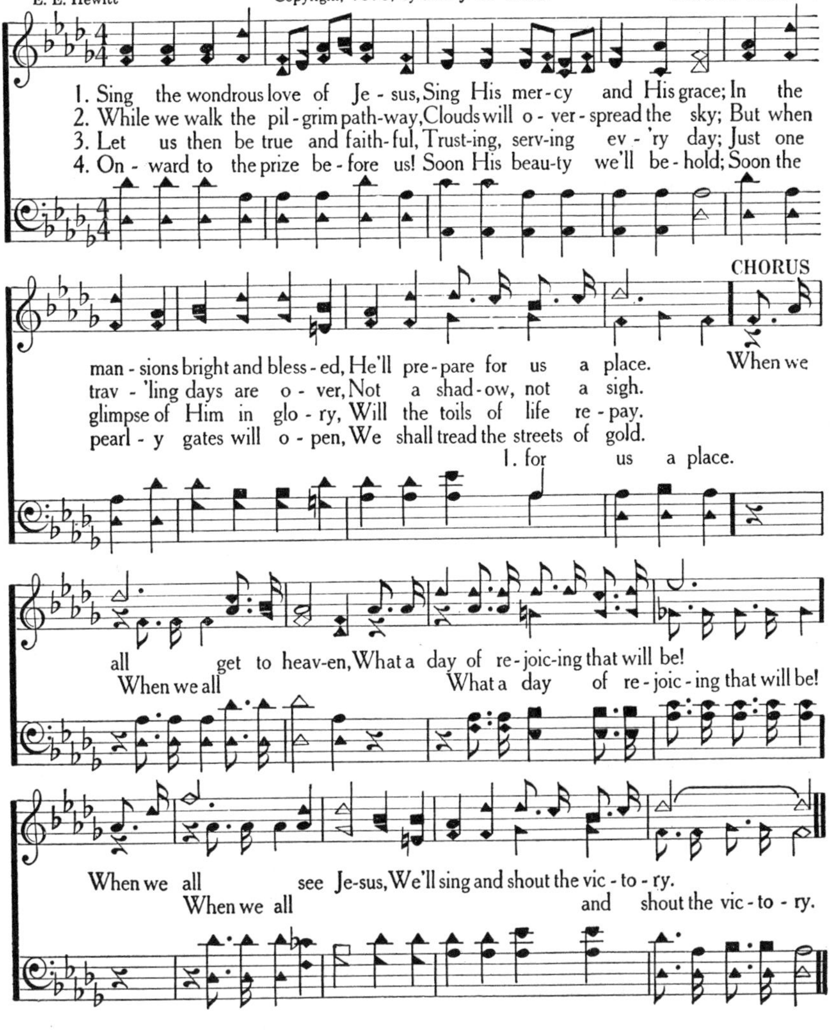

1. Sing the wondrous love of Je - sus, Sing His mer-cy and His grace; In the
2. While we walk the pil-grim path-way, Clouds will o - ver-spread the sky; But when
3. Let us then be true and faith-ful, Trust-ing, serv-ing ev - 'ry day; Just one
4. On - ward to the prize be - fore us! Soon His beau-ty we'll be - hold; Soon the

man - sions bright and bless - ed, He'll pre-pare for us a place.
trav - 'ling days are o - ver, Not a shad - ow, not a sigh.
glimpse of Him in glo - ry, Will the toils of life re - pay.
pearl - y gates will o - pen, We shall tread the streets of gold.

CHORUS

When we all get to heav-en, What a day of re - joic-ing that will be!
When we all   What a day of re - joic - ing that will be!

When we all see Je-sus, We'll sing and shout the vic - to - ry.
When we all   and shout the vic - to - ry.

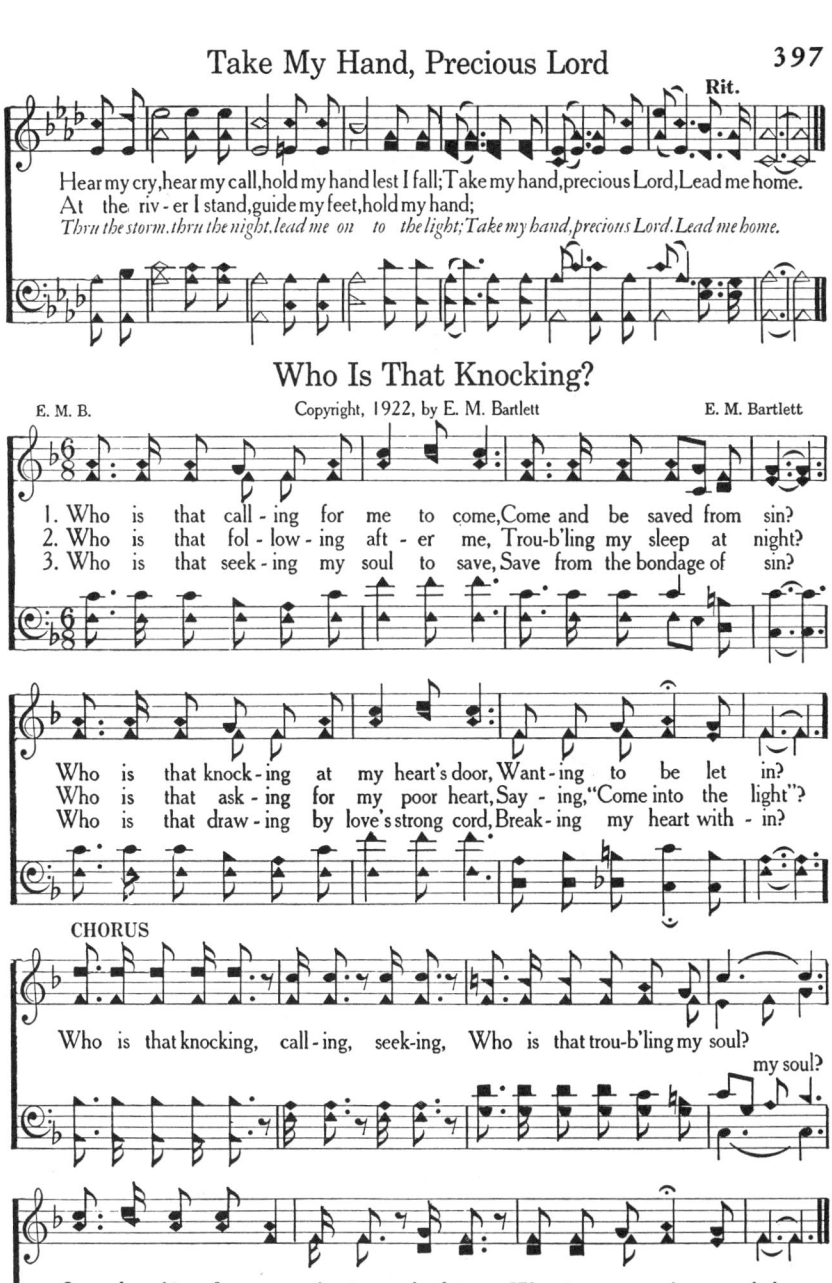

404 Heavenly Sunlight

Rev. H. J. Zelley
Copyright, 1899, by H. L. Gilmour
G. H. Cook

1. Walk-ing in sun-light all of my jour-ney, O-ver the mountains, thru the deep vale;
2. Shad-ows a-round me, shad-ows a-bove me, Nev-er con-ceal my Sav-ior and Guide;
3. In the bright sunlight ev-er re-joic-ing, Pressing my way to man-sions a-bove;

Je-sus has said I'll nev-er for-sake thee, Promise di-vine that nev-er can fail.
He is the light, in Him is no dark-ness, Ev-er I'm walk-ing close to His side.
Sing-ing His prais-es glad-ly I'm walk-ing, Walk-ing in sun-light, sun-light of love.

D. S.–Hal - le - lu - jah, I am re - joic - ing, Sing - ing His prais - es, Je - sus is mine.

CHORUS

Heav-en-ly sun-light, heav-en-ly sun-light, Flooding my soul with glo-ry di-vine;

Only Trust Him

J. H. S.
J. H. Stockton

1. Come ev-'ry soul by sin oppressed, There's mer-cy with the Lord,
2. For Je-sus shed His pre-cious blood, Rich bless-ings to be-stow;
3. Yes, Je-sus is the Truth, the Way, That leads you in-to rest;
4. Come, then, and join this ho-ly band, And on to glo-ry go;

And He will sure-ly give you rest, By trust-ing in His Word.
Plunge now in-to the crim-son flood, That wash-es white as snow;
Be-lieve in Him with-out de-lay, And you are ful-ly blest.
To dwell in that ce-les-tial land, Where joys im-mor-tal flow.

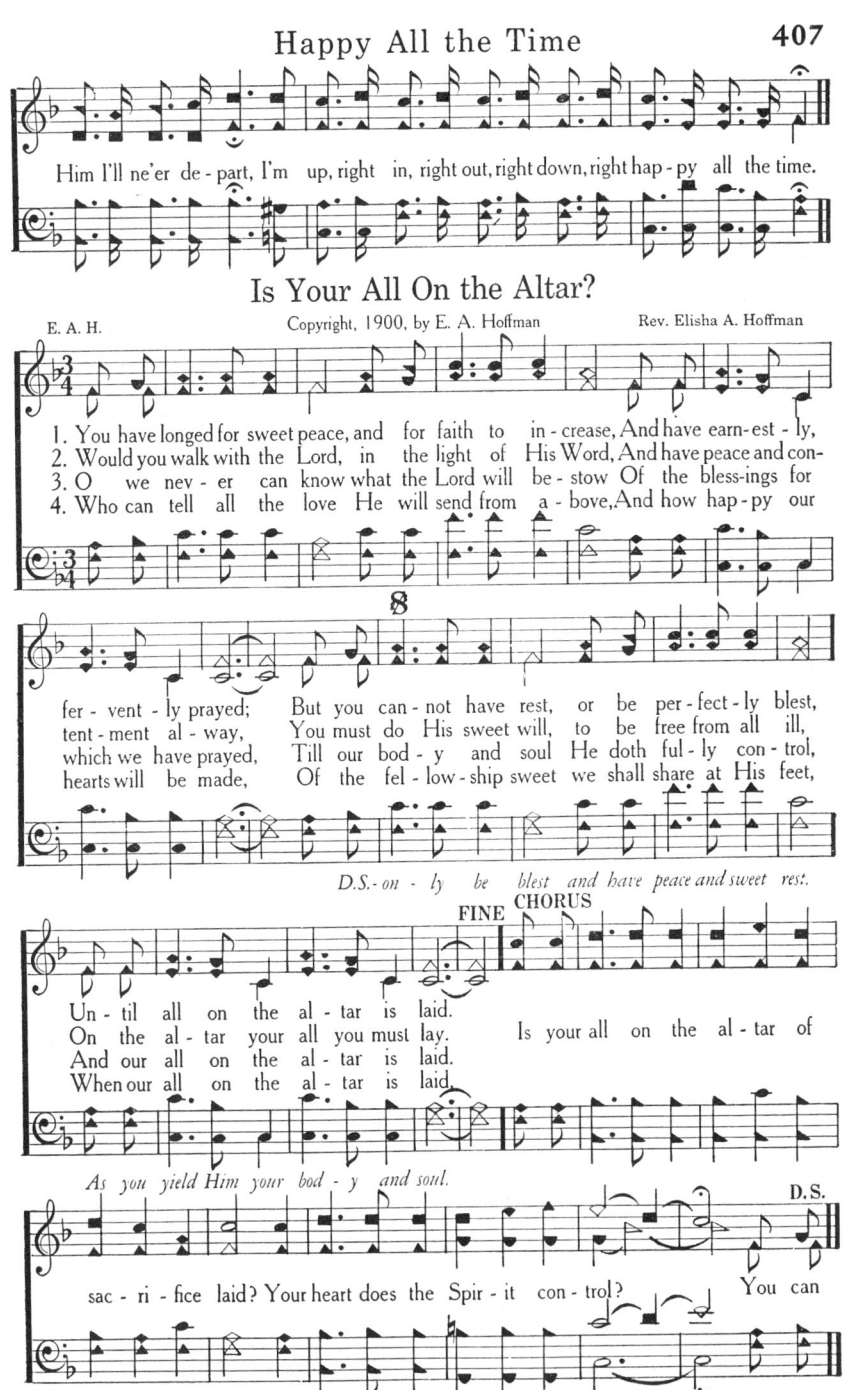

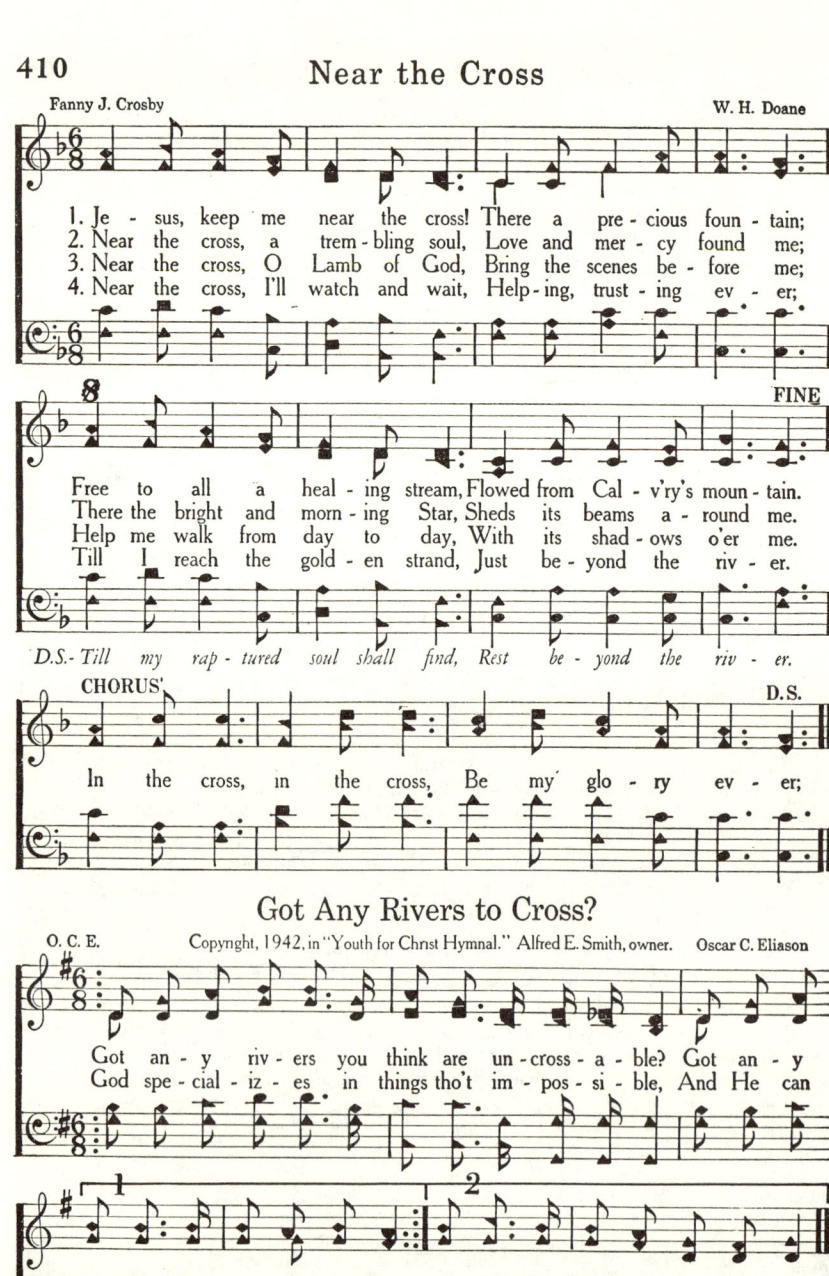

TOPICAL INDEX

BAPTISM

Blessed Assurance	181
Blest Be the Tie	75
Footprints of Jesus	47
He Leadeth Me	335
I Love to Walk With Jesus	186
I'll Have a New Life	134
I'm Glad I'm One of Them	249
I'm Going Thru, Jesus	123
Jesus, Lover of My Soul	63
Jesus Passed This Way Before	190

BLOOD

Are You Washed in the Blood?	177
At the Cross	264
His Blood Is on My Soul	101
Nothing But the Blood	368
Remember	274
The Old Rugged Cross	305
There Is a Fountain	379
There Is Power in the Blood	390
When I See the Blood	378
Wonderful Power in the Blood!	289

CHILDREN

Be a Light for Jesus	260
Give of Your Best to the Master	189
Happy All the Time	406
He Loves Me	355
I'll Fly Away	333
I'm on the Battlefield	268
Jesus Loves Me	87
Let It Shine on Me	338
Let My Life Be a Light	169
O Say, But I'm Glad	372
The B-I-B-L-E	332
This Little Light of Mine	342
Wonderful Words of Life	205

CHORUSES

Cleanse Me	141
Got Any Rivers to Cross?	410
Happy All the Time	406
Have Thine Own Way, Lord	375
I Feel Like Traveling On	133
I Have Forsaken All to Follow Jesus	340
I'll Be So Glad	348
I'm Happy With Jesus Alone	91
Just a Little Talk With Jesus	92
Let My Life Be a Light	169
O Say, But I'm Glad	372
Sunlight	271
Take My Hand, Precious Lord	396
The B-I-B-L-E	332
The Lord Will Make a Way for Me	398
This Is Like Heaven to Me	334
This Little Light of Mine	342
Victory in Jesus	120
Victory Today Is Mine	239
When We All Get to Heaven	393
Where Could I Go?	345

CHRISTMAS

Hark! the Herald Angels Sing	408
It Came Upon a Midnight Clear	399
Joy to the World	408
O Little Town of Bethlehem	371
Silent Night	366

CONSECRATION

All I Need	183
Deeper, Deeper	230
Fill My Way With Love	179
Footprints of Jesus	47
Hand in Hand With Jesus	55
Have Thine Own Way, Lord	375
He Leadeth Me	335
His Blood Is on My Soul	101
His Way With Thee	216
I Surrender All	354
I Want to Love Him More	342
I'm Glad I'm One of Them	249
Jesus Has Full Control	171
Lead Me Gently Home, Father	234
Near the Cross	410
Nothing Between	395
O How I Love Jesus	391
Waiting on the Lord	303
Where He Leads Me	65

EASTER

Christ Arose!	258
Hallelujah! We Shall Rise	272
He Lives	188

FUNERAL

Gathering Buds	383
I'll Meet You by the River	132
I'll Meet You in the Morning	14
Meet Me There	256
Nearer, My God, to Thee	67
No Tears in Heaven	367
O Think of the Home Over There	369
Precious Memories	93
Safe in the Arms of Jesus	403
Shall We Gather at the River?	384
That Glad Reunion Day	310
The Eastern Gate	312
The Haven of Rest	344
The Last Mile of the Way	382
The Pearly White City	126
We Are Going Down the Valley	302
We'll Never Say Good-by	402
What a Gathering That Will Be	299
When the Roll is Called Up Yonder	240
When They Ring the Golden Bells	294
Where We'll Never Grow Old	293
Will My Mother Know Me There?	291
Will We Be United There?	347

INVITATION

Almost Persuaded	392
Amazing Grace	57
Are You Washed in the Blood?	177
At the Cross	264
Come Unto Me	44
Don't Turn Him Away	326
Don't Wait Too Long	117
God Calling Yet	362
Have You Any Time for Jesus?	394
Is Thy Heart Right With God?	357
Is Your All on the Altar?	407
Jesus Is Calling	161
Jesus Is Passing This Way	215
Jesus Saves	91
Just As I Am	81
Kneel at the Cross	165
Leave It There	164
Let Him In	324
Nothing But the Blood	368

TOPICAL INDEX—Continued

O Don't Stay Away — 49
O, Why Not Tonight? — 370
Prepare to Meet Thy God — 321
Sin Can Never Enter There — 325
Softly and Tenderly — 385
Standing Outside — 148
There Is a Fountain — 379
There's a Great Day Coming — 380
Where Is My Boy Tonight? — 392
Where Shall I Be? — 405
Whosoever Will — 236
Why Do You Wait? — 378
You Can't Do Wrong and Get By — 354

JUDGMENT

God Holds the Future in His Hands — 259
Hallelujah! We Shall Rise — 272
In the Great Triumphant Morning — 261
My Record Will Be There — 104
The Great Judgment Morning — 208
The Great Reaping Day — 89

MISSIONARY

Be a Light for Jesus — 260
Be Ready to Go — 24
Bring Them In — 85
Carry On for Him — 267
Give of Your Best to the Master — 189
Hold the Fort — 400
I'll Go Where You Want Me to Go — 213
Keep on the Firing Line — 212
Rescue the Perishing — 145
Send Me — 48
Send the Light — 281
Stand Up for Jesus — 381
Throw Out the Life-Line — 388
Work, for the Night Is Coming — 377
Working for the Crown — 322

MOTHER

If I Could Hear My Mother Pray Again — 315
My Mother's Bible — 246
Sweetest Mother — 328
Take This Message to Mother — 195
Tell Mother I'll Be There — 194
Will My Mother Know Me There? — 291

PRAYER

Abide With Me — 61
He Prayed — 254
I Am Praying for You — 159
I Must Tell Jesus — 107
I Need the Prayers — 331
I Would Not Be Denied — 382
Just a Little Talk With Jesus — 92
Let Me Live Close to Thee — 250
Let My Life Be a Light — 169
Lord, Lead Me On — 96
Make Me a Blessing — 152
Only Give Me Jesus — 374
Pass Me Not — 373
Prayer-Bells of Heaven — 276

TESTIMONY

An Old Account Settled — 176
Gettin' Ready to Leave This World — 116
Glory Hallelujah in My Soul — 225
Hallelujah, I'm Going Home — 178
He Abides — 184
He Keeps Me Singing — 125
He Lives — 188
He Set Me Free — 235
He Whispers Sweet Peace to Me — 360
Heavenly Sunlight — 404
Heaven's Jubilee — 110
His Blood Is on My Soul — 101
I Am Determined to Hold Out — 156
I Am Thine, O Lord — 362
I Feel Like Traveling On — 133
I Have Found the Way — 314
I Have Somebody With Me — 313
I Know My Name Is There — 346
I Love to Tell the Story — 323
I Love to Walk With Jesus — 186
I Never Shall Forget the Day — 130
I Rejoice in the Lord — 266
I'm Free Again — 4
I'm Glad I Counted the Cost — 95
I'm Glad I'm One of Them — 249
I'm Going Thru, Jesus — 123
I've Got That Old Time Religion — 112
It Is Truly Wonderful — 226
It's Glory for Me — 262
Jesus Spoke to Me — 76
Love Lifted Me — 265
My Burdens Rolled Away — 284

GENERAL INDEX

A

A Beautiful Life	174
A Child of the King	348
A New Name in Glory	154
A Shelter in the Time of Storm	337
A Wonderful Time	175
Abide With Me	61
All Alone	227
All I Need	183
All Will Be Glory	182
Almost Persuaded	392
Amazing Grace	57
America	51
An Old Account Settled	176
Anchored in His Love	43
Are You Washed in the Blood?	177
At Calvary	139
At the Cross	264

B

Battle Hymn	229
Be a Light for Jesus	260
Be Ready to Go	24
Blessed Assurance	181
Blessed Be the Name	353
Blest Be the Tie	75
Bring Them In	85
Bringing in the Sheaves	109

C

Carry On for Him	267
Christ Arose!	258
Christ Receiveth Sinful Men	221
Cleanse Me	141
Come Unto Me	44
Consecration	77

D

Deeper, Deeper	230
Do You Ever Think to Pray?	136
Do You Know Him?	232
Don't Turn Him Away	326
Don't Wait Too Long	117
Drifting Too Far From the Shore	360

E

Echoes From the Glory Shore	210
Everybody Will Be Happy Over There	180
Ev'ry Day With Jesus	398

F

Faith of Our Fathers	99
Farther Along	409
Fill My Way With Love	179
Footprints of Jesus	47

G

Gathering Buds	383
Gettin' Ready to Leave This World	116
Give of Your Best to the Master	189
Glory Hallelujah in My Soul	225
Glory Is Coming	231
Glory to His Name	113
God Be With You	209
God Calling Yet	362
God Holds the Future in His Hands	259
God Leads Us Along	364
God Put a Rainbow in the Cloud	245
God's Message to Man	108
Got Any Rivers to Cross?	410
Grace for Every Need	56

H

Hallelujah, I'm Going Home	178
Hallelujah Side	237
Hallelujah! We Shall Rise	272
Hand in Hand With Jesus	55
Happy All the Time	406
Hark! the Herald Angels Sing	408
Have Faith in God	54
Have Thine Own Way, Lord	375
Have You Any Time for Jesus?	394
He Abides	184
He Is Able to Deliver Thee	352
He Keeps Me Singing	125
He Knows How	214
He Leadeth Me	335
He Lives	188
He Loves Me	355
He Prayed	254
He Set Me Free	235
He Whispers Sweet Peace to Me	360
He Will Be With Me	58
He'll Take Me Thru	68
He'll Understand	185
He'll Understand and Say "Well Done"	282
He's Coming	253
He's Coming Again	187
He's My King	20
Heavenly Sunlight	404
Heaven's Jubilee	110
Hide Me, Rock of Ages	193
Hide Thou Me	122
His Blood Is on My Soul	101
His Love	192
His Love and Glory Are Mine	60
His Love Lights the Way	317
His Way With Thee	216
Hold the Fort	400
Hold to God's Unchanging Hand	358
Holy, Holy	131
Honey in the Rock	338
How Beautiful Heaven Must Be	105
How Firm a Foundation	127

I

I Am Determined to Hold Out	156
I Am Praying for You	159
I Am So Glad	124
I Am Thine, O Lord	362
I Can, I Will, I Do Believe	79
I Can Tell You the Time	34
I Can't Feel at Home in This World	394
I Don't Want to Get Adjusted	218
I Fell Like Traveling On	133
I Have Forsaken All to Follow Jesus	340
I Have Found the Way	314
I Have Somebody With Me	313
I Hear Thy Welcome Voice	111
I Know He Heard My Prayer	16
I Know I Have Religion	366
I Know My Name Is There	346
I Know Whom I Have Believed	340
I Love the Lord Down in My Heart	8
I Love to Tell the Story	323
I Love to Walk With Jesus	186

GENERAL INDEX—Continued

I Must Tell Jesus ... 107
I Need the Prayers ... 331
I Need Thee Ev'ry Hour ... 330
I Never Shall Forget the Day ... 130
I Rejoice in the Lord ... 266
I Shall Not Be Moved ... 339
I Surrender All ... 354
I Want to Be a Worker ... 207
I Want to Know More About My Lord ... 6
I Want to Love Him More ... 342
I Will Never Turn Back ... 173
I Will Sing the Wondrous Story ... 228
I Will Slip Away Home ... 32
I Will Trade the Old Cross for a Crown ... 247
I Won't Have to Cross Jordan Alone ... 257
I Would Not Be Denied ... 382
I'd Like to Talk It Over With Him ... 42
I'd Rather Be an Old-Time Christian ... 46
I'll Be a Friend to Jesus ... 386
I'll Be Satisfied ... 135
I'll Be So Glad ... 348
I'll Be True ... 74
I'll Fly Away ... 333
I'll Go Where You Want Me to Go ... 213
I'll Have a New Life ... 134
I'll Live in Glory ... 202
I'll Live On ... 211
I'll Meet You by the River ... 132
I'll Meet You in the Morning ... 14
I'll Ride on the Clouds With My Lord ... 316
I'm Free Again ... 4
I'm Glad I Counted the Cost ... 95
I'm Glad I'm One of Them ... 249
I'm Going Home ... 45
I'm Going That Way ... 88
I'm Going Thru, Jesus ... 123
I'm Happy With Jesus Alone ... 91
I'm in a New World ... 94
I'm Living in Canaan Now ... 287
I'm Never Alone ... 80
I'm on the Battlefield ... 268
I'm on the Rock ... 356
I'm Winging My Way Back Home ... 219
I've Anchored in Jesus ... 275
"I've Been a Waitin'" ... 349
I've Got That Old Time Religion ... 112
I've Never Been Sorry ... 114
I've Seen the Light ... 242
If I Could Hear My Mother Pray Again ... 315
If Jesus Goes With Me ... 204
If We Never Meet Again ... 36
In That Home of the Soul ... 263
In the Great Triumphant Morning ... 261
In the Shadow of the Cross ... 115
In the Sweet Forever ... 50
Inside the Gate ... 40
Is It Well With Your Soul? ... 334
Is Thy Heart Right With God? ... 357
Is Your All on the Altar? ... 407
It Came Upon a Midnight Clear ... 399
It Is Love ... 172
It Is Truly Wonderful ... 226
It Won't Be Long ... 62
It's a Grand and a Glorious Feeling ... 28
It's Glory for Me ... 262
It's Just Like Heaven ... 2

J

Jehovah Is Leading You ... 191
Jesus Forgives and Forgets ... 336
Jesus Has Full Control ... 171
Jesus, Hold My Hand ... 52
Jesus, I'm Coming Some Day ... 163
Jesus Is Calling ... 161
Jesus Is Passing This Way ... 215
Jesus Is the One ... 273

Jesus Keeps Me Happy ... 243
Jesus, Lover of My Soul ... 63
Jesus Loves Even Me ... 59
Jesus Loves Me ... 87
Jesus Paid It All ... 119
Jesus Paid It All (New Arr.) ... 170
Jesus Passed This Way Before ... 190
Jesus Saves ... 97
Jesus, Savior, Pilot Me ... 53
Jesus Spoke to Me ... 76
Jesus, the Light of the World ... 396
Joy to the World ... 408
Joy Unspeakable ... 167
Just a Little Talk With Jesus ... 92
Just a Little While ... 140
Just As I Am ... 81
Just Because He Loved Me So ... 241
Just One Way to the Gate ... 66
Just Over in the Glory-Land ... 248
Just Over the Stars ... 244

K

Keep on the Firing Line ... 212
Kneel at the Cross ... 165

L

Land Where Living Waters Flow ... 98
Lead Me Gently Home, Father ... 234
Leaning on the Everlasting Arms ... 359
Leave It There ... 164
Leave Your Sorrows and Come Along ... 166
Let Him In ... 324
Let It Shine on Me ... 338
Let Me Live Close to Thee ... 250
Let My Life Be a Light ... 169
Let the Lower Lights Be Burning ... 402
Lift Me Up Above the Shadows ... 100
Living by Faith ... 162
Looking for a City ... 18
Looking This Way ... 387
Lord, I Believe ... 283
Lord, I'm Coming Home ... 153
Lord, Lead Me On ... 96
Love Lifted Me ... 265

M

Make Me a Blessing ... 152
Mansions in Heaven ... 160
Meet Me There ... 256
More About Jesus ... 103
Moving Higher ... 106
Music in My Soul ... 102
My Burdens Rolled Away ... 284
My Faith Looks Up to Thee ... 69
My Hope Is Built ... 390
My Jesus, I Love Thee ... 143
My Lord Will Care for Me ... 118
My Mother's Bible ... 246
My Record Will Be There ... 104
My Redeemer ... 311
My Reward ... 217
My Saviour First of All ... 320
My Sins Are Gone ... 318
My Song of Praise ... 155

N

Near the Cross ... 410
Nearer, My God, to Thee ... 67
Never Alone ... 288
No, Not One ... 365

GENERAL INDEX—Continued

No Tears in Heaven ... 367
Not Made With Hands ... 389
Nothing Between ... 395
Nothing But the Blood ... 368

O

O Come All Ye Faithful ... 388
O Don't Stay Away ... 49
O Happy Day ... 343
O Happy Day (New Arr.) ... 86
O How I Love Jesus ... 391
O, I Want to See Him ... 279
O Little Town of Bethlehem ... 371
O Say, But I'm Glad ... 372
O Think of the Home Over There ... 369
O, Why Not Tonight? ... 370
Old Camp-Meeting Days ... 252
Old Time Power ... 121
One at Last ... 84
Only Give Me Jesus ... 374
Only Trust Him ... 404
Onward, Christian Soldiers ... 372
Our Lord's Return to Earth ... 327

P

Pass Me Not ... 373
Praise Him! Praise Him! ... 151
Prayer-Bells of Heaven ... 276
Precious Memories ... 93
Prepare to Meet Thy God ... 321
Press Along to Glory-Land ... 147
Press Along, Weary Pilgrim, Press On ... 146
Press On, It Won't Be Long ... 374

R

Ready ... 386
Redeemed ... 277
Remember ... 274
Rescue the Perishing ... 145
Revive Us Again ... 370
Rock of Ages ... 83
Rock of Ages Keep My Soul ... 144

S

Safe in the Arms of Jesus ... 403
Saved by Grace ... 352
Saved, Saved! ... 224
Savior, More Than Life ... 400
Send Me ... 48
Send the Light ... 281
Shall We Gather at the River? ... 384
Silent Night ... 366
Sin Can Never Enter There ... 325
Sin Is to Blame ... 344
Since Jesus Came Into My Heart ... 269
Singing of Love Divine ... 82
Softly and Tenderly ... 385
Some Day ... 203
Some Glad Day ... 270
Stand By Me ... 149
Stand Up for Jesus ... 381
Standing on the Promises ... 329
Standing Outside ... 148
Sunlight ... 271

Sunshine in the Soul ... 222
Sweeping Through the Gates ... 280
Sweet By-and-By ... 350
Sweet Hour of Prayer ... 71
Sweetest Mother ... 328
Swing the Door Open Wide ... 332

T

Take a Moment and Live ... 26
Take It to the Lord in Prayer ... 307
Take Me as I Am ... 336
Take My Hand. Precious Lord ... 396
Take My Life and Let It Be ... 73
Take the Name of Jesus With You ... 376
Take This Message to Mother ... 195
Tell and Sing the News ... 278
Tell It to Jesus Alone ... 129
Tell Me the Story of Jesus ... 201
Tell Mother I'll Be There ... 194
That Glad Reunion Day ... 310
The B-I-B-L-E ... 332
The Comforter Has Come ... 406
The Dearest Friend I Ever Had ... 150
The Eastern Gate ... 312
The Glory-Land Way ... 286
The Great Judgment Morning ... 208
The Great Physician ... 363
The Great Reaping Day ... 89
The Harder the Battle, the Sweeter ... 128
The Haven of Rest ... 344
The Healing Waters ... 309
The Land of Perfect Day ... 22
The Last Mile of the Way ... 382
The Life-Boat ... 308
The Lily of the Valley ... 285
The Lord Is With Me ... 72
The Lord Will Make a Way for Me ... 398
The Love of God ... 220
The Meeting in the Air ... 10
The Old Gospel Ship ... 306
The Old Rugged Cross ... 305
The Old-Time Religion ... 351
The Pearly White City ... 126
The Promised Land ... 376
The Royal Telephone ... 304
The Son Hath Made Me Free ... 158
The Unclouded Day ... 401
There Is a Fountain ... 379
There Is Power in the Blood ... 390
There Shall Be Showers of Blessing ... 384
There's a Bridge O'er the River ... 301
There's a God Somewhere ... 142
There's a Great Day Coming ... 380
There's a Guiding Hand ... 38
This Is Like Heaven to Me ... 334
This Little Light of Mine ... 342
Throw Out the Life-Line ... 388
'Tis So Sweet to Trust in Jesus ... 137
Too Late to Pray ... 255
Trust and Obey ... 157
Twilight Is Falling ... 346
'Twill Be Glory By and By ... 233

V

Victory in Jesus ... 120
Victory Today Is Mine ... 239

W

Waiting on the Lord ... 303
Waiting Up There ... 206
Watching You ... 368

GENERAL INDEX—Continued

We Are Going Down the Valley — 302
We Shall See the King — 300
We'll Never Say Good-by — 402
We'll Reap What We Sow — 330
We'll Soon Be Done With Troubles ... 30
We'll Understand It Better By and By 251
We'll Work Till Jesus Comes — 361
"Well Done, My Child" — 70
What a Friend We Have — 341
What a Gathering That Will Be — 299
What a Happy Time — 298
What a Wonderful Feeling — 297
When God Dips His Love in My Heart 138
When He Calls I'll Fly Away — 12
When He Put a Little Sunshine In — 78
When I Get to the End of the Way — 238
When I Make My Last Move — 295
When I See the Blood — 378
When Jesus Comes in the Clouds — 296
When Jesus Shall Reign — 90
When My Name Is Called in Glory — 168
When Our Lord Shall Come Again — 200
When the Home Gates Swing Open — 223
When the Redeemed Are Gathering In 319
When the Roll Is Called Up Yonder — 240
When They Ring the Golden Bells — 294
When We All Get to Heaven — 393
Where Could I Go? — 345
Where He Leads Me — 65
Where Is My Boy Tonight? — 392
Where Milk and Honey Flows — 292
Where Shall I Be? — 405
Where the Soul Never Dies — 199
Where We'll Never Grow Old — 293
While the Years Roll On — 197
Whispering Hope — 198
Who Is That Knocking? — 397
Whosoever Will — 236
Why Do You Wait? — 378
Will Jesus Find Us Watching? — 364
Will My Mother Know Me There? — 291
Will We Be United There? — 347
Will You Meet Me Over Yonder? — 196
Wonderful Grace of Jesus — 64
Wonderful Peace — 290
Wonderful Power in the Blood! — 289
Wonderful Story of Love — 356
Wonderful Words of Life — 205
Won't It Be Wonderful There? — 358
Work, for the Night Is Coming — 377
Working for the Crown — 322

Y

Yield Not to Temptation — 380
You Can't Do Wrong and Get By — 354
You Never Mentioned Him to Me — 350